GOVERNMENT PROCEDURES AND OPERATIONS

THE FOREIGN EARNED INCOME TAX EXCLUSION FOR INDIVIDUALS

ANALYSES AND ALTERNATIVES

GOVERNMENT PROCEDURES AND OPERATIONS

Additional books in this series can be found on Nova's website under the Series tab.

Additional e-books in this series can be found on Nova's website under the e-book tab.

GOVERNMENT PROCEDURES AND OPERATIONS

THE FOREIGN EARNED INCOME TAX EXCLUSION FOR INDIVIDUALS

ANALYSES AND ALTERNATIVES

MOLLY MILBURN
EDITOR

nova publishers
New York

Library of Congress Cataloging-in-Publication Data

ISBN: 978-1-63321-974-8

Published by Nova Science Publishers, Inc. † New York

CONTENTS

PREFACE

For tax year 2011 (the most recent data available), an estimated 445,000 tax returns claimed the foreign earned income exclusion (FEIE), which is 0.3 percent of all individual tax returns filed. Taxpayers were able to exclude from taxable income about $30 billion in foreign earned income and housing costs, with about 45 percent excluding all or most of their foreign earned income. The FEIE reduces the tax liability of U.S. taxpayers working abroad even if they paid no foreign income taxes to another country. U.S. taxpayers in higher tax countries can eliminate their U.S. tax liability using the foreign tax credit, which is intended to prevent double taxation when foreign income is taxed by both the United States and a foreign country. This book describes the number and types of taxpayers using the tax expenditure, and analyzes how the tax expenditure may interact with other provisions of the tax code, such as the foreign tax credit; describes what is known about how the tax expenditure may affect business decisions about the employment of U.S. workers abroad, and U.S. exports; and evaluates the potential advantages and disadvantages of modifying or removing the tax expenditure.

Chapter 1 - Since 1926, special tax benefits have been available for U.S. citizens working abroad. Internal Revenue Code section 911—which cost an estimated $4.4 billion in 2013— provides a tax exclusion for foreign earned income, as well as an exclusion and deduction for foreign housing costs. GAO was asked to assess section 911.

This report (1) describes the number and types of taxpayers using the tax expenditure, and analyzes how the tax expenditure may interact with other provisions of the tax code, such as the foreign tax credit; (2) describes what is known about how the tax expenditure may affect business decisions about the employment of U.S. workers abroad, and U.S. exports; and (3) evaluates the potential advantages and disadvantages of modifying or removing the tax expenditure.

To address these objectives, GAO analyzed 2011 IRS statistical data; reviewed the tax code and relevant government and academic literature; and interviewed government officials, experts, and stakeholders, including groups representing citizens working abroad and employers. As its criteria for good tax policy, this report uses GAO's tax expenditures evaluation guide, *Tax Expenditures: Background and Evaluation Criteria and Questions,* GAO-13-167SP.

Chapter 2 - For 2011, the total amount of foreign-earned income reported on Form 2555, Foreign Earned Income, by nearly 450,000 U.S. taxpayers was $54.2 billion. This represented growth in real terms of 32.3 percent since 2006, the last year a study was prepared on these data. Asian-based U.S. taxpayers reported the largest amount of total foreign-earned income ($24.9 billion) from any continent, a 52.2-percent increase in real growth from the $16.4 billion reported for 2006. In addition, U.S. taxpayers claimed more than $28.3 billion as a foreign-earned income exclusion on their tax returns for the year. Between 2006 and 2011, the inflation-adjusted amount of the foreign-earned income exclusion increased 38.4 percent, while the housing exclusion increased 5.8 percent, rising from just under $1.5 billion to nearly $1.6 billion for 2011.

Foreign-source gross income reported by U.S. taxpayers on Form 1116, Foreign Tax Credit, reached nearly $170.0 billion for 2011. In real terms, this represents a 27.0-percent growth in foreign-source gross income from 2006. By region, European-based taxpayers reported the most foreign-source gross income ($32.4 billion) and the country with the highest foreign-source gross income ($13.9 billion) was the United Kingdom. Foreign taxes paid or accrued, also reported on Form 1116, were $22.0 billion and total foreign tax credit, claimed on approximately 6.9 million returns, was just under $16.5 billion, an inflation adjusted 34.5-percent growth from 2006.

In: The Foreign Earned Income Tax Exclusion ISBN: 978-1-63321-974-8
Editor: Molly Milburn

Chapter 1

TAX POLICY: ECONOMIC BENEFITS OF INCOME EXCLUSION FOR U.S. CITIZENS WORKING ABROAD ARE UNCERTAIN*

United States Government Accountability Office

WHY GAO DID THIS STUDY

Since 1926, special tax benefits have been available for U.S. citizens working abroad. Internal Revenue Code section 911—which cost an estimated $4.4 billion in 2013— provides a tax exclusion for foreign earned income, as well as an exclusion and deduction for foreign housing costs. GAO was asked to assess section 911.

This report (1) describes the number and types of taxpayers using the tax expenditure, and analyzes how the tax expenditure may interact with other provisions of the tax code, such as the foreign tax credit; (2) describes what is known about how the tax expenditure may affect business decisions about the employment of U.S. workers abroad, and U.S. exports; and (3) evaluates the potential advantages and disadvantages of modifying or removing the tax expenditure.

To address these objectives, GAO analyzed 2011 IRS statistical data; reviewed the tax code and relevant government and academic literature; and

* This is an edited, reformatted and augmented version of the United States Government Accountability Office publication, GAO-14-387, dated May 2014.

interviewed government officials, experts, and stakeholders, including groups representing citizens working abroad and employers. As its criteria for good tax policy, this report uses GAO's tax expenditures evaluation guide, *Tax Expenditures: Background and Evaluation Criteria and Questions,* GAO-13-167SP.

WHAT GAO RECOMMENDS

GAO made no recommendations in this report. IRS and Treasury provided technical comments that were incorporated as appropriate. Commerce said it had no comments.

WHAT GAO FOUND

For tax year 2011 (the most recent data available), an estimated 445,000 tax returns claimed the foreign earned income exclusion (FEIE), which is 0.3 percent of all individual tax returns filed. About 17 percent of FEIE filers also claimed the foreign housing exclusion or deduction. Over half of FEIE filers reported working for a foreign employer, and less than one-third reported working for a U.S. company; the balance reported working as self-employed or for other entities. Taxpayers were able to exclude from taxable income about $30 billion in foreign earned income and housing costs, with about 45 percent excluding all or most of their foreign earned income. The FEIE reduces the tax liability of U.S. taxpayers working abroad even if they paid no foreign income taxes to another country. U.S. taxpayers in higher tax countries can eliminate their U.S. tax liability using the foreign tax credit, which is intended to prevent double taxation when foreign income is taxed by both the United States and a foreign country.

While tax costs could influence employment for some U.S. workers overseas, there is little evidence the tax expenditure affects exports. A few studies have asserted the tax expenditure benefits U.S. exports. For example, this would happen if the expenditure encouraged U.S. companies to hire more Americans abroad by making it cheaper for them to do so, and if Americans working abroad promoted exports through the nature of their work and other activities. The extent to which the tax expenditure influences employment of U.S. workers abroad and U.S. exports depends on several factors, including the role of tax-related costs in hiring decisions and whether workers are involved in activities contributing to U.S. export promotion. Experts and stakeholders GAO interviewed expressed differing views on the emphasis employers place on specific overseas hiring factors. While about half of those GAO interviewed said that employers make overseas hiring decisions based first on the candidates' qualifications, or that the cost of prospective employees was not a primary consideration, about half also told us the added tax costs of employing U.S. citizens could influence some employment decisions. Most experts interviewed stated that the tax expenditure's effect on exports is likely small at most.

In terms of good tax policy, there is room for debate regarding how potential revisions to the current tax expenditure may affect choices about where to work and who to hire. The current tax expenditure may have positive and negative effects on both the efficient allocation of labor resources and on equity. The magnitude of these effects is unknown, making it unclear whether the tax expenditure provides any net economic benefits. These uncertainties also make it difficult to draw definite conclusions about certain policy alternatives. Repealing the tax expenditure would reduce the tax inducement for U.S. citizens to relocate to lower tax countries, but would also make U.S. citizens more costly for any employer to hire than citizens of most other countries, which do not tax foreign earned income. Removing the maximum limit ($99,200 for 2014) for the exclusion would eliminate the tax cost differential with other countries, but would allow high-income individuals to avoid U.S. taxes on foreign earned income. Targeted tax relief may be justified for extreme cost of living areas, and the design of any alternative would affect the complexity for taxpayers and the Internal Revenue Service (IRS), as well as the federal tax cost.

ABBREVIATIONS

AGI	adjusted gross income
CBO	Congressional Budget Office
Commerce	Department of Commerce
CRS	Congressional Research Service
FEIE	foreign earned income exclusion
FTC	foreign tax credit
IRC	Internal Revenue Code
IRS	Internal Revenue Service

JCT	Joint Committee on Taxation
OMB	Office of Management and Budget
SOI	Statistics of Income
Treasury	Department of the Treasury

***

May 20, 2014

The Honorable Jim McDermott
House of Representatives

The Honorable Michael Honda
House of Representatives

The Honorable Carolyn Maloney
House of Representatives

The United States taxes its citizens on their worldwide income, regardless of where they reside. Since 1926, certain special tax benefits have been available for U.S. citizens working abroad. Section 911 of the Internal Revenue Code (IRC) permits a tax exclusion for foreign earned income, as well as an exclusion or deduction for foreign housing costs. Because section 911 reduces income tax liability through special tax provisions, both the Department of the Treasury (Treasury) and the Joint Committee on Taxation (JCT) identify section 911 as a tax expenditure. The costs and benefits of this tax expenditure have been the subject of policy and economic discussion. Some have defended the tax expenditure on the grounds that it enables U.S. workers overseas to better compete for jobs with non-U.S. foreign nationals (who typically pay no taxes on overseas earned income) and that it thereby encourages the overseas employment of Americans, who play an important role in promoting exports. However, others have highlighted that some of these claims lack evidence, or are based on outdated assumptions, given changes in the global economy over the past several decades. From a tax policy perspective, some have debated whether or not the tax expenditure provides economic and other benefits to the United States when compared to its costs.

Our previous work has shown that, once enacted, tax expenditures—special tax credits, deductions, exclusions, exemptions, deferrals, and preferential tax rates—and their relative contributions toward achieving federal missions and goals are often less visible than spending programs, which are subject to more systematic review.[1] One reason for this is that in practice, tax expenditures often operate like entitlement programs not subject to annual appropriations. Since 1994, we have recommended greater scrutiny of tax expenditures, as periodic reviews could help determine how well specific tax expenditures work to achieve their goals and how their benefits and costs compare to those of spending programs with similar goals. In prior reports, we have described how program evaluations could be conducted to measure progress toward achieving a program's intended purpose.[2] Even if a tax expenditure is meeting its intended purpose, broader questions can be asked about its effects beyond that purpose. Specifically, the long-standing criteria of economic efficiency, fairness, transparency, simplicity, and administrability can be used to evaluate whether a tax expenditure is good tax policy.[3]

You asked us to examine section 911—the foreign earned income exclusion (FEIE) as well as an exclusion or deduction for foreign housing costs. Specifically, this report (1) describes the number and types of taxpayers using the tax expenditure, and analyzes how the tax expenditure may interact with other provisions of the tax code, such as the foreign tax credit; (2) describes what is known about how the tax expenditure may affect business decisions about the employment of U.S. workers abroad, and U.S. exports; and (3) evaluates the potential advantages and disadvantages of modifying or removing the tax expenditure.

To describe the number and types of taxpayers using section 911, we analyzed Internal Revenue Service (IRS) Statistics of Income Division (SOI) publications and obtained aggregated data tabulations for individual tax returns for tax year 2011 (the most recent year available). Our analysis of SOI statistical data is subject to sampling errors because the SOI data set is based on a sample of tax returns as filed and does not reflect IRS audit results or any net operating loss carrybacks from future years.[4] To assess the reliability of the data we analyzed, we reviewed IRS documentation and interviewed agency officials familiar with the data. We determined that these data were sufficiently reliable for the purposes of this report. To determine how the tax expenditure may interact with other provisions of the tax code, we reviewed the Internal Revenue Code, IRS guidance, and tax advisor literature to analyze how the tax expenditure affects eligibility for other income tax provisions.

To determine what is known about how the tax expenditure may affect business decisions about the employment of U.S. workers abroad, and U.S.

exports, we reviewed related literature and available information on business practices used in employing U.S. citizens abroad, including government reports, academic literature, and surveys. We also interviewed Department of Commerce (Commerce) officials as well as nine experts and nine stakeholders.[5] (We define stakeholders as individuals or groups who may offer a valuable perspective on how the tax expenditure may affect business decisions concerning the employment of U.S. workers abroad, and exports, but who may also have a vested interest in the issue.) We selected experts based on various factors, including their affiliation with leading higher education or research institutions and their publication or research experience associated with the FEIE or related topics, such as international taxation, international business strategy, trade, or U.S. labor. One consideration in the selection process was to talk with experts whose views varied from one to another. We selected a range of stakeholder organizations that represent the interests of relevant entities, such as U.S. citizens working overseas and U.S. businesses. Appendix I provides more information on the experts and stakeholders we interviewed.

To evaluate options to modify or remove the tax expenditure, we reviewed a variety of sources, including studies by GAO, the Congressional Research Service (CRS), JCT, Treasury, IRS, the Taxpayer Advocate, and other government reports as well as academic literature on the tax expenditure and related options. We also interviewed the nine experts and nine stakeholders discussed above on the advantages and disadvantages of modifying the tax expenditure. We used the tax expenditure evaluation guide we developed to evaluate the performance of the FEIE and possible options for modifying or removing it.[6] This report focuses on the guide's criteria for evaluating whether the tax expenditure is good tax policy and meets its purpose, namely,

- Does the tax expenditure generate net economic benefits for society?
- Is the tax expenditure fair and equitable?
- Is the tax expenditure transparent, simple, and administrable?
- How well does the tax expenditure achieve its purpose?

The tax policy criteria may sometimes conflict with one another; in addition, some are subjective. As a result, there are likely to be trade-offs between the criteria when evaluating a particular tax expenditure. We also considered how the federal budget is affected by the tax expenditure and how the budget would be affected by options to modify or remove the tax expenditure. We analyzed Treasury's tax expenditure estimates from1986 to 2014, and reviewed available JCT estimates and interviewed JCT staff about the revenue effects of modifying the tax expenditure. Detailed information on our scope and methodology can be found in appendix I.

We conducted this performance audit from July 2013 to May 2014 in accordance with generally accepted government auditing standards. Those standards require that we plan and perform the audit to obtain sufficient, appropriate evidence to provide a reasonable basis for our findings and conclusions based on our audit objectives. We believe that the evidence obtained provides a reasonable basis for our findings and conclusions based on our audit objectives.

BACKGROUND

The United States requires its citizens and resident aliens, regardless of where they reside, to file U.S. tax returns and pay federal income taxes on their worldwide income.[7] To prevent double taxation on foreign source income, U.S. citizens and resident aliens are allowed a credit or deduction against U.S. tax for foreign income taxes paid to other countries—the foreign tax credit (FTC).[8] Under section 911 of the tax code, U.S. citizens who live and work abroad are also permitted an exclusion of foreign earned income and an exclusion or deduction of certain foreign housing costs.[9] In contrast to U.S. policy, most other countries do not tax their citizens if they reside in a country other than their country of citizenship.

Exclusion for Foreign Earned Income and Exclusion or Deduction for Foreign Housing Costs

The income that U.S. citizens and resident aliens may exclude under section 911 is generally limited to amounts earned for services performed abroad, including salaries and wages (except wages from the U.S. government[10]). It does not include income derived from capital, such as interest, dividends, capital gains, or retirement distributions.[11] To qualify for the FEIE, the U.S. citizen or resident alien's tax home[12] must be in a foreign country[13] and, if a U.S. citizen, must be a bona fide resident[14] of a foreign country or countries for an uninterrupted period which includes an entire taxable year or, if a U.S. citizen or resident alien, must be physically present in a foreign country for at least 330 days over a 12-month period.[15]

As shown in figure 1, tax legislation enacted since 1986 has changed the maximum amount of foreign earned income that can be excluded from federal income taxation. Since 2006, the exclusion amount has been indexed for inflation. For 2014, the amount is $99,200. Taxpayers claiming the FEIE may also be eligible to claim an exclusion or deduction for foreign housing costs. Taxpayers may claim the exclusion if their employers paid their housing costs, or they may claim the deduction if their housing costs were paid from self-employment earnings.[16] Housing expenses must exceed a base amount of 16 percent of the maximum FEIE for the tax year, computed on a daily basis for the number of days in the qualifying period that falls within the tax year.[17] For 2014, the base housing amount is $15,872 (16 percent of $99,200), or $43.48 per day. Since 2006, foreign housing expenses in excess of the base that are eligible for the housing exclusion or deduction have been limited generally to 30 percent of the maximum FEIE; however, the maximum has varied depending on the location of the home. Treasury was given the authority to raise the maximum housing exclusion to reflect actual housing costs in higher-cost foreign cities.[18]

The amendments to the FEIE in 2006 changed the taxation of income exceeding the exclusion by imposing a stacking rule. Amounts claimed under the exclusions for foreign earned income and foreign housing costs reduce taxable income, and a taxpayer does not owe U.S. income taxes on the amounts excluded. For taxpayers that have taxable income after claiming the FEIE and foreign housing exclusion, the applicable tax rate is determined by calculating taxable income without taking these exclusions into account.[19] This stacking rule results in taxpayers who claim FEIE exclusions being subject to the same marginal tax rates as taxpayers with the same level of income who are not eligible for (or do not elect to claim) the exclusions.[20]

IRS collects data on use of the FEIE on Form 2555, *Foreign Earned Income*, filed with the taxpayer's income tax return.[21] Taxpayers who have income within the exclusion limit, are not self-employed, and do not claim the foreign housing exclusion or deduction may file the 2555-EZ. IRS publishes some aggregate information on the FEIE in its annual statistical publication.[22] Every 5 years, IRS augments its sample and publishes a mandated study with additional detail about taxpayers claiming the FEIE.[23] Prior special studies—the last study based on 2006 tax data was published in 2009[24]—show that the FEIE has been claimed on an increasing number of tax returns. IRS plans to issue the 2011 tax year study during 2014.

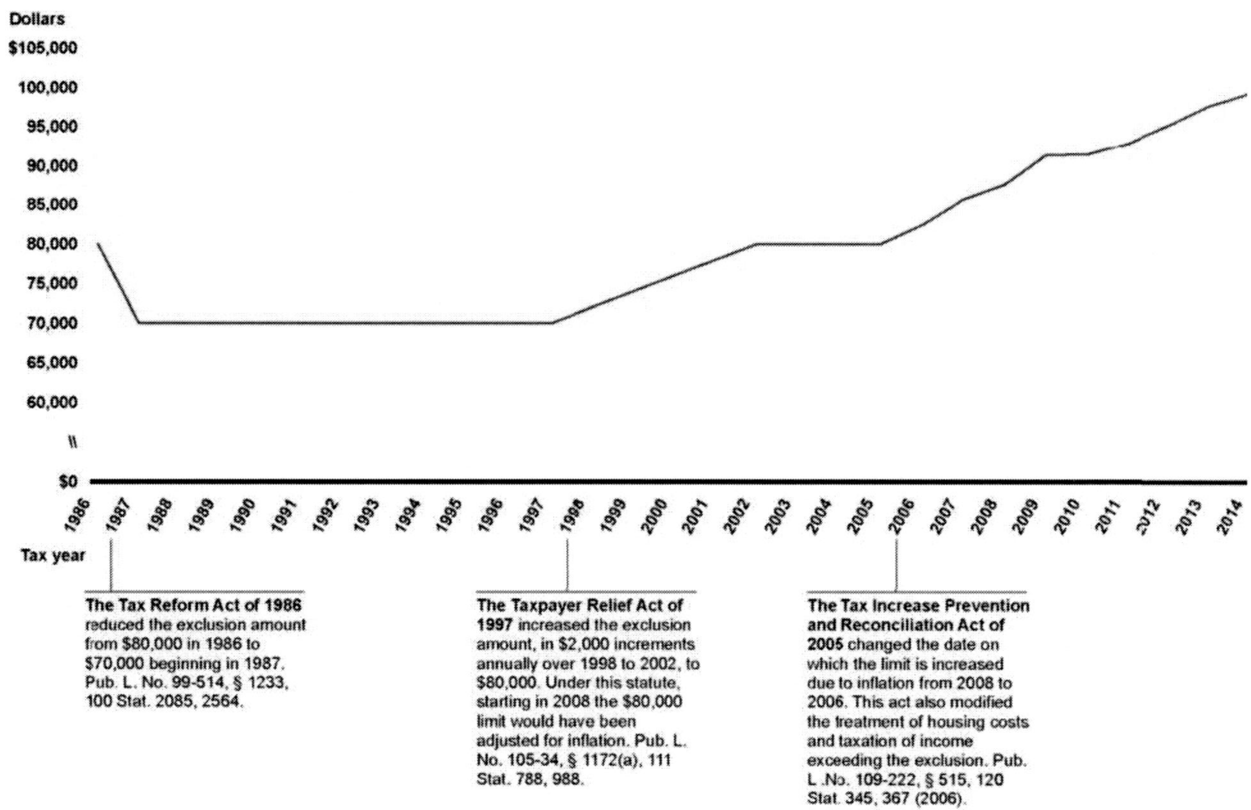

Source: GAO analysis of public laws.

Figure 1. Effect of Tax Legislation on the Amount of the Foreign Earned Income Exclusion (1986-2014).

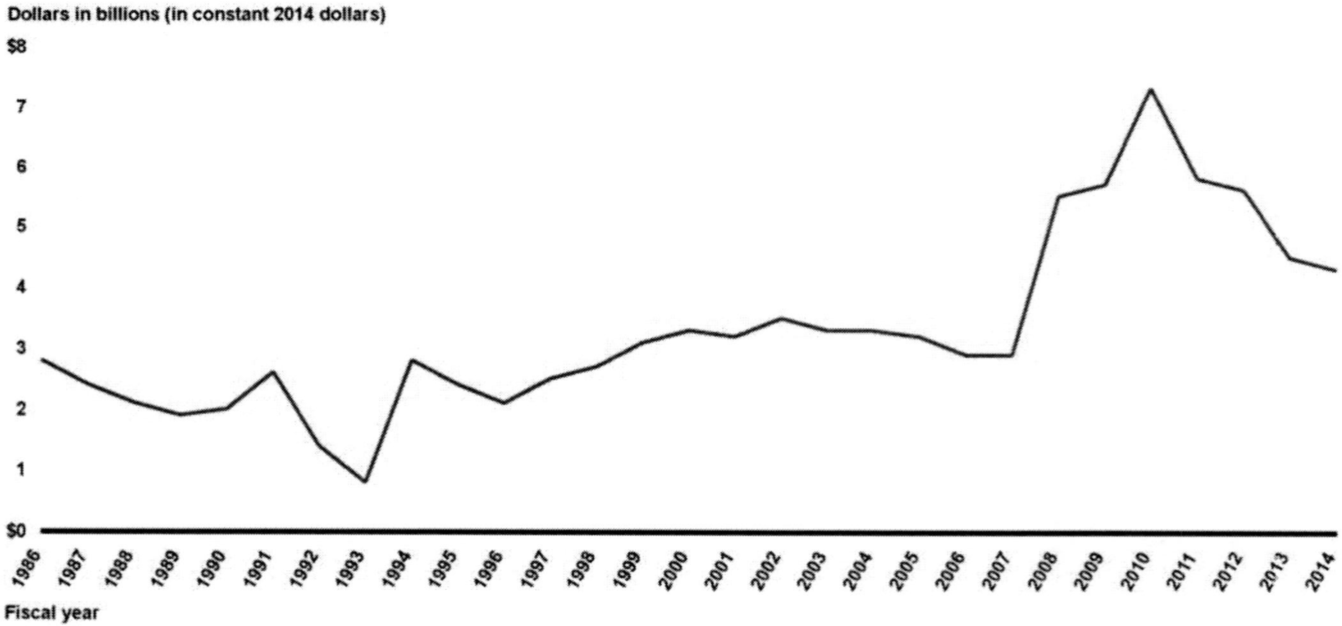

Source: GAO analysis of OMB budget reports on tax expenditure, fiscal years 1986-2015.

Note: Changes in economic conditions and estimation techniques can affect revenue loss estimates for tax expenditures, making them differ from year to year. Also, legislation affecting tax rates or the tax structure affects tax expenditure estimates. When statutory rates increase, a taxpayer's ability to avoid tax on a portion of income is worth more; consequently, tax expenditures are worth more. Likewise, when rates decrease, tax expenditures are worth relatively less.

Figure 2. Tax Expenditure Revenue Loss Estimates (Fiscal Years 1986-2014).

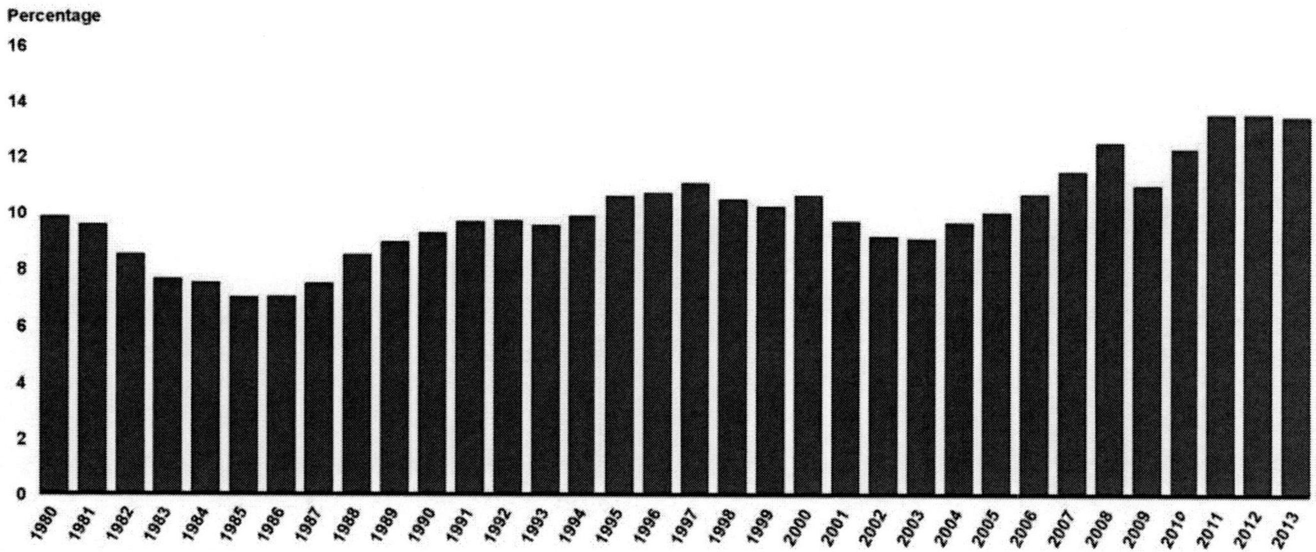

Source: GAO analysis of Bureau of Economics Analysis data.

Figure 3. Share of Exports in U.S. Gross Domestic Product, 1980-2013.

Treasury and JCT both calculate the estimated revenue losses for the tax expenditure assuming that all other parts of the tax code remain constant and taxpayer behavior is unchanged. [25] Both tax expenditure estimates assume that taxpayers would be allowed to use the next best tax treatment and claim the FTC. Tax expenditure estimates do not incorporate any behavioral responses and thus do not represent the amount of revenue that would necessarily be gained if the tax expenditure was repealed.[26] Figure 2 shows the revenue losses estimated by Treasury for the tax expenditure since 1986.[27] For 2014, Treasury estimated revenue losses of $4.3 billion (about 0.4 percent of the sum of all tax expenditures), and JCT estimated revenue losses of $5 billion for the FEIE and $1 billion for the foreign housing costs.[28] The revenue forgone through tax expenditures requires higher tax rates to raise any given amount of revenue, reduces resources available to fund other federal activities, increases the budget deficit, or reduces any budget surplus.

Employment Overseas and Exports

Historically, the tax expenditure has been defended on the grounds that it encourages the employment of U.S. workers abroad who play an important role in promoting U.S. exports.[29] Companies use international assignments for various reasons, such as to fill managerial or technical gaps, or to transfer skills to local staff. U.S. and foreign-owned companies have reported growth in international assignments in the past few years, according to survey data concerning global relocation trends.[30] According to the same survey data, international assignees are increasingly scattered globally, with a growing number of assignments in emerging markets such as Southeast Asia and Africa.

According to data from Commerce's Bureau of Economic Analysis, U.S. exports have increased in the past few decades, growing at a rate of about 7 percent between 1980 and 2013. [31] During that period, exports as a share of U.S. gross domestic product fluctuated, reaching the highest level in the last few years (see figure 3).

While U.S. exports have grown, the value of imported intermediate goods used in their production has also increased. The nature of export production, particularly in the manufacturing sector, has changed in recent decades. For example, according to literature on global trade, factors such as more efficient global communication and transportation systems have made it easier for companies to allocate their production globally to take advantage of lower input prices, including labor cost. These factors also have facilitated the flow of intermediate production inputs across global supply chains, creating more integrated manufacturing. In turn, the foreign content of U.S. exports has increased from the 1990s to 2000s.

In recent years the administration has emphasized export promotion as a high priority for the federal government. In 2010, President Obama launched the National Export Initiative via Executive Order. The initiative is aimed at doubling the dollar value of U.S. exports by the end of 2014.[32] The Office of Management and Budget subsequently identified the National Export Initiative's goal of doubling U.S. exports as one of 14 interim crosscutting priority goals under the GPRA Modernization Act of 2010.[33] We have reported that federal agencies that promote exports face coordination and management challenges, which could hinder their effectiveness in supporting the initiative's goal.[34] Concurrent with the release of the President's fiscal year 2015 budget, the administration released new crosscutting goals which focus on new priorities.[35] However, according to information on Performance.gov, the cross-agency effort to double exports will remain an administration priority, and efforts related to this goal will continue to be led by the Export Promotion Cabinet and the Trade Promotion Coordinating Committee. Export promotion also continues to be an agency goal for the Department of Commerce.

RELATIVELY FEW INDIVIDUAL TAXPAYERS CLAIMED THE FOREIGN EARNED INCOME EXCLUSION, AND CLAIMING IT IS MORE BENEFICIAL THAN THE FOREIGN TAX CREDIT FOR THOSE IN LOWER TAX COUNTRIES

A Relatively Small Number of Tax Returns Claimed the Foreign Earned Income Exclusion and over Half Reported Working for Foreign Employers

In tax year 2011 (the most current data available), the FEIE was claimed on an estimated 445,000 tax returns, which is 0.3 percent of about 145 million individual tax returns filed that year. We could not estimate the FEIE filers as a share of U.S. citizens abroad or the subset of citizens working abroad because reliable population figures are not available.36 An estimated 45 percent of returns claiming the FEIE were married filing jointly (where one or both spouses may have claimed the FEIE), and 36 percent were single filers.37

As shown in figure 4, an estimated 17 percent38 of filers claiming the FEIE also claimed the foreign housing exclusion or foreign housing deduction.

The number of tax returns claiming the FEIE has increased since the early 1990s, as shown in figure 5. During this period, the total number of individual tax returns filed also increased.

Over half of Form 2555 filers in 2011 reported that their employer was a foreign entity (including foreign affiliates of U.S. companies). Less than one-third reported that their employer was a U.S. company, and the balance reported working as self-employed or for other entities. Taxpayers self-report the type of employer they work for, based on IRS guidance. IRS had not published information on the type of employer in its 5-year special studies, but data provided by IRS show that the employer pattern was generally consistent over the 2001, 2006, and 2011 studies.

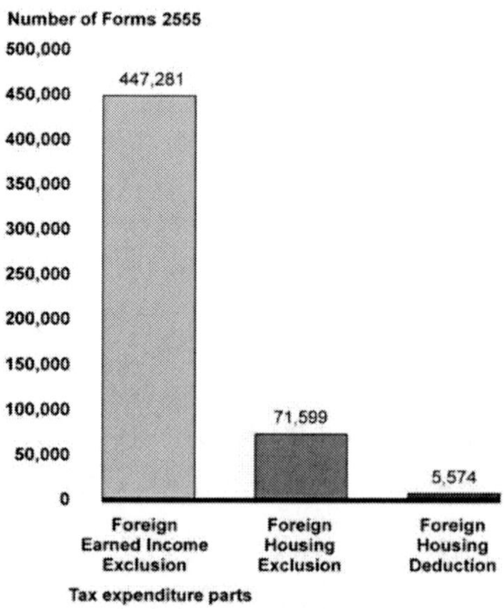

Source: GAO analysis of IRS Statistics of Income 2011 data.

Note: Taxpayers may file up to two Forms 2555. When comparing the number of tax returns claiming these amounts in IRS's Publication 1304 to the number of Forms 2555 filed, the difference was less than one percent. Estimates for the number of returns with a FEIE, foreign housing exclusion, and foreign housing deduction, respectively, have 95 percent confidence intervals that are within 14 percent of the estimate itself.

Figure 4. Estimated Number of Forms 2555 with the Foreign Earned Income Exclusion, Housing Exclusion, and Housing Deduction, Tax Year 2011.

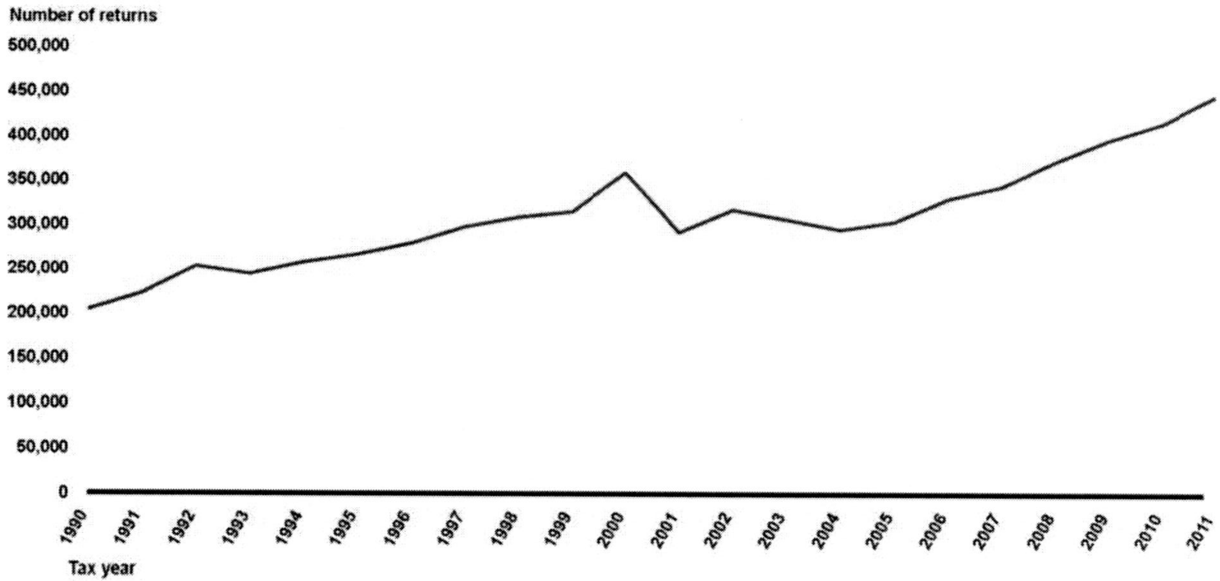

Source: GAO analysis of IRS Statistics of Income data, tax years 1990-2011.

Note: Estimates for the number of returns claiming the foreign earned income exclusion (FEIE) by year, from 1992 to 2011, have 95 percent confidence intervals that are within 12 percent of the estimate itself. Estimates for the number of all Forms 1040 filed by year, from 1992 to 2011, have 95 percent confidence intervals that are within 0.2 percent of the estimate itself. The sampling errors for the estimates of the number of returns claiming the FEIE and the number of all 1040 filers in 1990 and 1991 were not available. Given almost 20 subsequent years of such estimates with available sampling errors, we report the estimated number of filers overall and who claim the FEIE for these 2 years without assessing the margins of error, but do not make any statistical comparisons for 1990 and 1991.

Figure 5. Estimated Number of Returns Claiming the Foreign Earned Income Exclusion (Tax Years 1990- 2011)

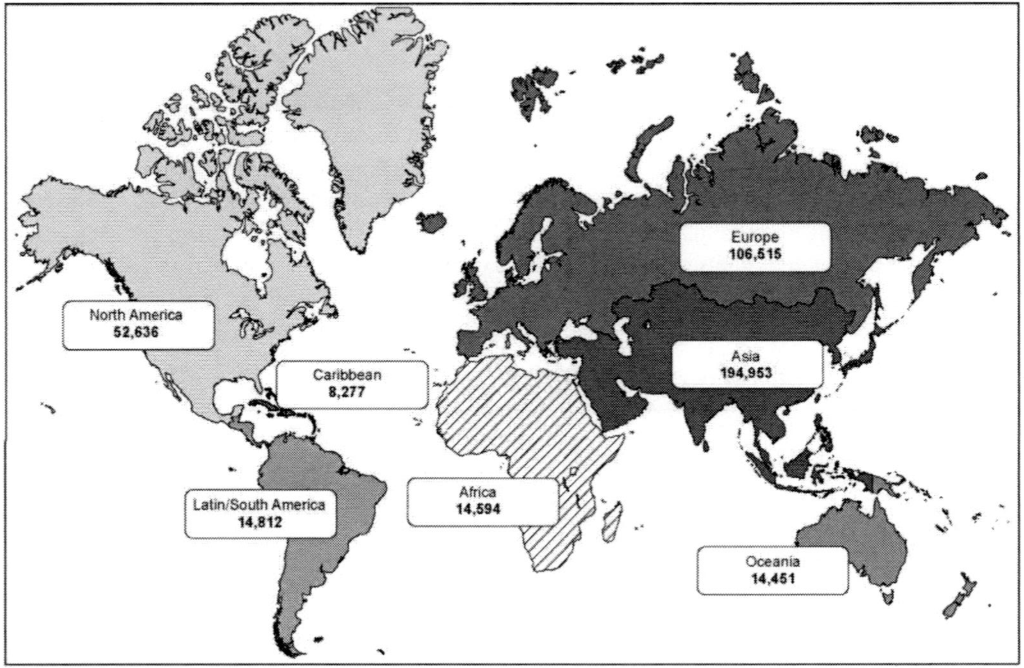

Source: GAO analysis of IRS Statistics of Income 2011 data.

Note: All other countries not counted in the region totals accounted for 42,311 tax returns. Estimates for the number of returns with foreign earned income filed with geographic regions Asia, Europe, and North America have 95 percent confidence intervals that are within 10 percent of the estimate itself. All other regions and other countries have 95 percent confidence intervals that are within 20 percent except for the Caribbean, which is within 24.65 percent of the estimate itself.

Figure 6. Estimated Number of Forms 2555 with Foreign Earned Income Filed by Geographic Region, Tax Year 2011.

In tax year 2011, about two-thirds of Form 2555 filers were in Asia (43 percent) and Europe (24 percent); see figure 6. Canada and the United Kingdom have relatively large numbers of Form 2555 filers; see table 1.

Some Filers Were Able to Exclude All Income, and Foreign Earned Income Exclusion Filers Had Higher Average Income and Lower U.S. Tax Rates than the Average Form 1040 Filer

In tax year 2011, taxpayers claimed about $30 billion for the FEIE, foreign housing exclusion, and foreign housing deduction.[39] About 45 percent of FEIE 2555 filers had an adjusted gross income (AGI) of less than $10,000, as shown in table 2. This reflects that some taxpayers were able to exclude all or most of their foreign earned income in calculating their AGI.

Taxpayers claiming the FEIE had higher average income ($163,450) than the average Form 1040 filer ($58,706), as shown in table 3.[40]

Table 1. Estimated Number of Forms 2555 with Foreign Earned Income Filed by Countries with the Most Filings, Tax Year 2011

Country	Region	Number of Forms 2555
Canada	North America	45,740
United Kingdom	Europe	30,861
Japan	Asia	23,073
Afghanistan	Asia	22,987
China	Asia	22,362
Germany	Europe	19,091
Iraq	Asia	13,938
South Korea	Asia	13,671
Hong Kong	Asia	13,274
United Arab Emirates	Asia	12,126

Source: GAO analysis of IRS Statistics of Income 2011 data.

Note: While Canada and the United Kingdom have more estimated filings than the other countries (and Canada is higher than the United Kingdom), the number of forms filed are not necessarily statistically different among the remaining eight countries.

Table 2. Comparison of Estimated Distribution of Returns for the FEIE and All Form 1040s, Tax Year 2011

Adjusted gross income	Distribution of returns claiming FEIE	Distribution of all 1040 returns
No adjusted gross income	23.5	1.7
$1 under $10,000	21.9	15.9
$10,000 under $25,000	11.3	24.1
$25,000 under $50,000	11.3	23.7
$50,000 under $200,000	21.9	31.4
$200,000 under $1,000,000	8.8	3.0
$1,000,000 or more	1.2	0.2
All returns	100.0	100.0

Source: GAO analysis of IRS Statistics of Income 2011 data.

Note: Percentage estimates have 95 percent confidence intervals that are within 1 percentage point of the estimate itself. Totals for all returns may not add to 100 due to rounding.

Table 3. Comparison of Estimated Income of Returns for the FEIE and All Form 1040s, Tax Year 2011

Adjusted gross income	Average income of FEIE filers	Average income of all 1040 filers
Under $25,000	$55,409	$9,011
$25,000 under $50,000	$109,239	$36,497
$50,000 under $200,000	$182,680	$92,604
$200,000 under $1,000,000	$505,453	$344,323
$1,000,000 or more	$2,932,212	$3,187,604
All returns	$163,450	$58,706

Source: GAO analysis of IRS Statistics of Income 2011 data.

Note: The average income of FEIE filers with adjusted gross income of $25,000 under $50,000 has a 95 percent confidence interval that is within 11 percent of the estimate itself.

For the average U.S. tax rate (based on U.S. income tax amounts), taxpayers claiming the FEIE had lower average U.S. tax rates (6.8 percent) than all Form 1040 filers (12.3 percent), as shown in table 4. Table 4 also shows that while the average U.S. tax paid by FEIE filers is lower than the average tax paid by U.S. 1040 filers in all AGI categories, the average total tax paid—including both U.S. and foreign income taxes—by FEIE filers is lower than U.S. 1040 filers only among taxpayers with AGIs less than $50,000. In tax year 2011, 24 percent of taxpayers filing Forms 2555 also filed for the FTC.

The Foreign Earned Income Exclusion Is More Beneficial than the Foreign Tax Credit for U.S. Taxpayers in Lower Tax Countries

Depending on their earned income and the tax rate of the foreign country where they live and work, U.S. taxpayers may choose to use the FEIE, the FTC, or a combination of both to reduce their U.S. tax liability.[41] In low tax countries, the FEIE is more beneficial to taxpayers than the FTC. In high tax countries, the FTC may be more beneficial. This is illustrated in table 5 where we compare the U.S. income tax liability for a U.S. employee working in the United States to U.S. citizens working in three hypothetical countries with differing tax rates. In countries with no income tax (country A) a citizen using only the FEIE would owe no U.S. taxes on earned income up to the exclusion maximum. The same citizen using only the FTC would have the same U.S. tax liability and total taxes as the employee in the United States. In countries with lower tax rates than the United States (country B), a citizen using only the FEIE would owe no U.S. taxes. Using only the FTC, the same citizen would owe less U.S. taxes but the same total taxes as the employee in the United States. In countries with a higher tax rate than the United States (country C), the citizen has no U.S. income tax liability in either case.[42]

As illustrated above, some U.S. citizens working abroad have no foreign income tax liability because they live and work in countries that do not have income taxes. Other U.S. citizens working abroad may also face no or reduced foreign taxes. Some tax treaties may reduce tax liabilities for U.S. citizens abroad. For example, U.S. students, teachers, and trainees may be exempt from a treaty country's income tax. Workers of international organizations and nonprofits also may be exempt in some treaty countries. Some countries have introduced special tax incentives broadly targeted to attract or retain high-skilled workers—such as scientists, researchers and engineers—to locate in otherwise high-tax jurisdictions.[43] U.S. citizens in these situations benefit from the exclusion similar to taxpayers in lower tax countries and may have no or reduced foreign taxes to claim under the foreign tax credit method.

Table 4. Comparison of Estimated Tax Rates for Returns Claiming FEIE to All Form 1040 Returns, Tax Year 2011

Adjusted gross income	Average U.S. tax rate of FEIE filers	Average U.S. tax rate of all 1040 filers	Average total tax rate of FEIE filers	Average total tax rate of all 1040 filers
Under $25,000	0.2	2.3	0.3	2.3
$25,000 under $50,000	2.1	5.1	3.0	5.1
$50,000 under $200,000	6.7	10.4	10.4	10.4
$200,000 under $1,000,000	9.4	20.5	22.1	20.8
$1,000,000 or more	11.4	23.0	26.9	23.9
All returns	6.8	12.3	14.6	12.5

Source: GAO analysis of IRS Statistics of Income 2011 data.

Note: The average U.S. tax rate is based on income tax amounts. The average total tax rate is based on income tax amounts plus the FTC. Worldwide income was used for income tax amounts for FEIE filers, and total income was used for all 1040 filers. Percentage estimates for tax rates have 95 percent confidence intervals within 10 percent of the estimate itself, except for estimates for the average U.S. tax rate of FEIE filers with AGI of $25,000 under $50,000, which has a confidence interval within 11 percent of the estimate itself.

Excluded Income Counts in Determining Eligibility for Tax Benefits with Income Limits

U.S. citizens and resident aliens living outside the United States generally are allowed the same deductions and tax credits as citizens and residents living in the United States. For example, taxpayers living abroad who itemize can claim deductions for mortgage interest and real estate property taxes paid for owner-occupied homes. However, taxpayers claiming the FEIE are not eligible for the earned income tax credit.[44] To prevent double dipping, a taxpayer cannot deduct, exclude, or claim a credit for any item that can be allocated to or charged against the foreign earned income excluded.[45] For example, if a taxpayer in 2013 had $90,000 of foreign earned income, took the FEIE, and had $7,000 of moving expenses, the taxpayer could not claim any deductions allocable to her foreign earned income (including the moving expenses on her tax return) because she excluded all of her foreign earned income. However, if the taxpayer made more in foreign earned income than the FEIE limit, then she would be eligible to deduct the portion of the moving expenses allocable to the foreign earned income in excess of the FEIE limit.

Table 5. Comparison of the FEIE and FTC by Hypothetical Country, Tax Year 2013

Country where U.S. taxpayer resides and earns income[a]	United States	Country A No income tax	Country B Income tax lower than the United States	Country C Income tax higher than the United States
Earned income	$107,600	$107,600	$107,600	$107,600
Less: Standard deduction $6,100 and one exemption $3,900	($10,000)	($10,000)	($10,000)	($10,000)
U.S. taxable income without FEIE	$97,600	$97,600	$97,600	$97,600
Using FEIE only				
U.S. taxable income with FEIE	$97,600	$0	$0	$0
Foreign income tax	$0	$0	$10,670	$26,900
U.S. income tax	$20,628	$0	$0	$0
Total worldwide income tax	$20,628	$0	$10,760	$26,900
Effective foreign income tax rate	0%	0%	10%	25%
Effective (residual) U.S. income tax rate	19%	0%	0%	0%
Effective worldwide income tax rate	19%	0%	10%	25%
Using FTC only				
U.S. taxable income without FEIE	$97,600	$97,600	$97,600	$97,600
Foreign income tax	$0	$0	$10,760	$26,900
U.S. income tax after foreign tax credit	$20,628	$20,628	$9,868	$0

Table 5. (Continued)

Country where U.S. taxpayer resides and earns income[a]	United States	Country A No income tax	Country B Income tax lower than the United States	Country C Income tax higher than the United States
Total worldwide income tax	$20,628	$20,628	$20,628	$26,900
Effective foreign income tax rate	0%	0%	10%	25%
Effective (residual) U.S. income tax rate	19%	19%	9%	0%
Effective worldwide income tax rate	19%	19%	19%	25%

Source: GAO.

Notes: For each example, we computed the effective income tax rates by dividing the corresponding income taxes by earned income. Some U.S. citizens may face no or lower tax rates in a foreign country as a result of tax treaty benefits or special arrangements for workers of international organizations and nonprofits.

[a] This comparison includes certain assumptions, including that each employee (1) holds the same qualifications, (2) receives the same income, (3) has a single tax filing status, (4) would pay the same tax rates as local citizens of the hypothetical country, and (5) does not claim the foreign housing exclusion or deduction.

In determining applicable tax rates and eligibility for some tax provisions, excluded foreign earned income is added back in when calculating a modified adjusted gross income for certain tax credits and deductions that phase out (gradually limited until eliminated) at higher levels of income. For example, the excluded income is counted in determining eligibility for tax benefits which help pay for higher education, such as the American opportunity tax credit, lifetime learning credit, and student loan interest deduction. (Appendix II lists tax code provisions that interact with section 911.) When excluded amounts are added back in to calculate income eligibility for tax benefits and to determine marginal tax rates for included income, then taxpayers claiming the exclusion are in the same tax position as those taking the FTC on total foreign earned income.

U.S. TAX COSTS COULD INFLUENCE SOME U.S. OVERSEAS EMPLOYMENT DECISIONS, THOUGH THERE IS LITTLE EVIDENCE THE TAX EXPENDITURE AFFECTS EXPORTS

The FEIE's effects on hiring U.S. workers abroad and on exports can depend on various factors. Experts and stakeholders we interviewed expressed varying views on the emphasis employers place on certain overseas hiring factors, such as tax costs. Most experts we interviewed told us there was little evidence to indicate the tax expenditure could have more than a limited effect on exports.

The Tax Expenditure's Effects on Hiring of U.S. Workers Abroad and Exports Depends on Various Factors

A few studies that we reviewed for this report asserted that the tax expenditure leads to more Americans working abroad, which in turn increases U.S. exports.[46] For example, this could happen if the tax expenditure encouraged U.S. companies to hire more Americans abroad by making it cheaper to do so, and if Americans abroad promoted exports through the nature of their work and other activities. However, because the tax expenditure applies to workers employed by any type of employer, it could also increase the number of Americans working abroad for employers other than U.S. companies and their affiliates or subsidiaries. Those workers could affect U.S. exports adversely by working for foreign competitors or by facilitating imports.

However, the extent to which the tax expenditure influences employment of U.S. workers abroad and U.S. exports can depend on a number of factors, which can vary across different settings, according to articles we reviewed and the experts and stakeholders we interviewed (see figure 7).

For example, the extent to which the tax expenditure may encourage companies to hire U.S. citizens abroad can be influenced by the degree to which companies prioritize costs, including tax-related costs, compared to other factors, when making hiring decisions. This relationship can also be influenced by companies' preference for U.S. workers, compared to non-U.S. employees, when staffing certain positions abroad, or by the foreign tax rates in different foreign countries where certain jobs are located. Similarly, the tax expenditure's relationship to U.S. exports can be influenced by the extent to which Americans working abroad are employed by U.S. companies or by foreign entities. As noted earlier, many U.S. workers abroad do not work for U.S. companies, and may affect U.S. exports adversely.

The relationship can also be influenced by the extent to which U.S. workers abroad have jobs directly relating to export promotion, such as selling products or making sourcing decisions, or the extent to which they are more or less likely to purchase goods or materials from U.S. suppliers compared to foreign competitors. Finally, broader factors such as changes in overseas assignment patterns and information technology advances can affect the tax expenditure's relationship to the hiring of Americans abroad and exports. For example, information technology improvements that make it easier to communicate and access information remotely can influence the extent to which companies assign employees overseas, or the nature of these assignments.

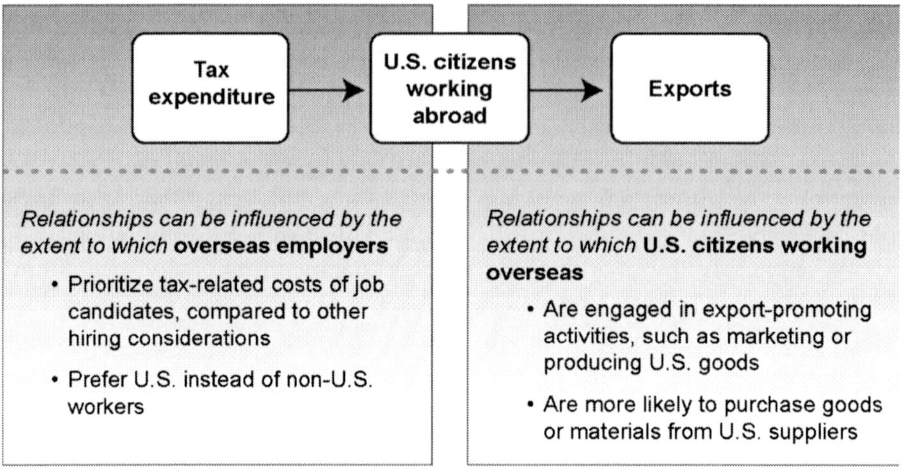

Source: GAO.

Figure 7. Various Factors Can Influence the Tax Expenditure's Relationship to U.S. Citizens Working Abroad and Exports.

Tax-Related Costs Could Influence Employment for Some U.S. Citizens Abroad in Certain Locations

U.S. Workers Abroad Can Incur a Higher Overall Tax Liability Than Non-U.S. Workers in Some Cases

U.S. overseas workers' tax costs can vary across locations, and in some cases can exceed the tax liabilities of non-U.S. workers. An employee on an employer-sponsored international assignment may receive allowances and reimbursements for housing and other expenses. These allowances can vary across locations, depending on local housing and other costs of living. The increased compensation causes the employee's income to be higher than when working in the United States, and can move the employee into a higher tax bracket. For illustrative purposes, table 6 compares the tax liability of a U.S. worker with that of a non-U.S. worker, at different income levels and with application of the FEIE, in a hypothetical country (which is not the home country of a non-U.S. worker) that has a lower effective tax rate than the United States. The example assumes the non-U.S. worker is not taxed by his or her home country on foreign-earned income; as we noted previously, the citizens of most other countries are not taxed by their country of citizenship if they reside in another country.[47] As table 6 shows, the FEIE can eliminate the U.S. income tax liability for some taxpayers residing overseas with foreign earned income. At higher income levels, taxpayers could incur a U.S. tax liability after applying the FEIE, which could result in an overall tax liability greater than that of non-U.S. workers who have the same earned income but are not taxed on income earned abroad.

The additional U.S. tax liability illustrated in table 6 could result in different actual after-tax income for U.S. employees, depending on whether and how companies adjust compensation. For example, some companies may increase compensation to fully or partially offset the U.S. employee's additional tax costs in order to attract U.S. citizens to work abroad. A company's willingness to do so could be shaped by the value it places on U.S. workers—its demand for U.S. overseas labor—relative to non-U.S. workers. A U.S. employee's willingness to work abroad—to supply U.S. overseas labor—could be influenced by how his or her after-tax income in the foreign country would compare to his or her after-tax income in the United States. According to survey data, most U.S. and foreign-owned companies use a tax equalization policy for their overseas assignees.[48] Under such a policy, employers pay their employees to cover higher taxes on working overseas than the employee would have been paid if they worked in the United States.

Table 6. Comparison of Tax Costs of U.S. and Non-U.S. Workers under the Foreign Earned Income Exclusion in a Hypothetical Host Country and at Different Income Levels

Nationality of employee[a]	**U.S.**	**Non-U.S.**	**U.S.**	**Non-U.S.**
Earned income[b]	$107,600	$107,600	$175,000	$175,000
Less FEIE	$97,600	N/A	$97,600	N/A
Less: standard deduction $6,100 and one exemption $3,900	$10,000	$10,000	$10,000	$10,000
Host country effective tax rate	10%	10%	10%	10%
Host country income tax	$10,760	$10,760	$17,500	$17,500
U.S. effective tax rate c	19%	N/A	23%	N/A
U.S. income tax after FEIE	$0	N/A	$18,865	N/A
U.S. income tax after Foreign Tax Credit	N/A	N/A	$9,105[d]	N/A
Total income after tax	$107,600	$107,600	$148,395	$157,500
Difference between U.S. worker after-tax income and that of a non-U.S. worker	**$0**	**N/A**	**-$9,105**	**N/A**

Source: GAO analysis.

Notes: This comparison includes certain assumptions, including that each employee (1) holds the same qualifications, (2) receives the same income, and (3) has a single tax filing status. The example also assumes the non-U.S. employee is not taxed by his or home country on foreign-earned income.

[a] The comparison focuses on home country tax rates for U.S. citizens and non-U.S. foreign nationals. U.S. citizens and non-U.S. foreign nationals would generally face the same local taxes as local citizens of the hypothetical host country.

[b] Housing costs are not explicitly included in the example. Differences in housing costs can be offset by applicable housing exclusions or deductions. However, in some cases the differences in housing costs can affect overall tax liability.

[c] The U.S. effective tax rate listed is that which applies to the earned income level provided in the example, without application of the tax expenditure.

[d] A U.S. citizen in this circumstance could also claim the foreign tax credit with respect to income that was not excluded using the foreign earned income exclusion.

Experts and Stakeholders Have Varying Views on the Emphasis Employers Place on Certain Overseas Hiring Factors

Experts and stakeholders expressed differing views on the emphasis or value employers place on certain overseas hiring factors. In particular, about half of the experts and stakeholders we interviewed said that employers make hiring decisions concerning overseas assignments based first on the candidates' job skills or qualifications, or that the cost of prospective employees was not a primary consideration. Specifically,

- One expert told us that in most cases involving senior-level employees, companies will first try to find the right person for the position, and then address cost and compensation issues.
- One stakeholder told us his firm's experience indicated costs were just one of several key hiring criteria used by most large companies, and that taxes were just one element of cost considerations, alongside costs for education, housing, and other expenses that could be associated with a given employee.

Nonetheless, about half of the experts and stakeholders we interviewed told us the additional tax costs of employing U.S. citizens could in some cases influence employment decisions; of these, two stakeholders told us tax costs were a predominant reason why some companies were hiring fewer Americans overseas. Specifically,

- One expert stated that skill-wise, the broadening of the global education base has made non-U.S. workers more competitive with U.S. workers in recent decades, creating more opportunities for companies to select less costly (yet equally skilled) foreign nationals over Americans.
- Related to that point, one stakeholder noted that certain large multinational firms have identified pools of qualified job candidates from different countries around the world; when compelled by cost considerations, they will hire from this pool.

Experts and stakeholders also noted that companies' preference for, and the value of, U.S. employees could vary across different situations. While about half of the stakeholders we interviewed said that U.S. citizens overseas have value for companies, compared to non-U.S. employees, about half of the experts we interviewed said such a value may be limited to certain types of jobs or companies and may not exist in certain contexts. Specifically,

- About half of the stakeholders we interviewed asserted there is a value in having Americans abroad, or that Americans are better able to facilitate U.S. companies' business transactions with foreign entities abroad than are non-U.S. employees.
- Several experts and a stakeholder stated that U.S. employees may have particular value for certain positions or for certain U.S. companies. For example, new companies without established trade partners or companies with American identities or interests, such as military contractors or companies in the entertainment industry, may have greater demand for U.S. employees.
- About half of the experts and several stakeholders said that in some cases U.S. workers had little or no comparative value relative to equally capable non-U.S. employees, such as for global companies, or that some companies may prefer hiring local citizens for certain positions.

Most Experts Interviewed See Little Evidence the Tax Expenditure Affects Exports

Most experts we interviewed and Commerce officials stated there was little evidence to indicate the tax expenditure could have more than a limited effect on exports. As noted previously, a few studies have asserted that the tax expenditure affects U.S. exports through effects on the number of Americans working abroad. Some articles have also asserted that exports in turn lead to increases in U.S. employment and to reductions in the trade deficit, justifying the tax expenditure. Moreover, stakeholders we interviewed offered examples of ways Americans abroad can promote exports, including by facilitating trade, purchasing source materials from U.S. suppliers, and advertising U.S. products. However, most experts we interviewed stated that it is difficult to determine the tax expenditure's effect on exports, or that there is little evidence to suggest any effect would be significant. Moreover, none of the experts we interviewed said they believed the tax expenditure was likely to have a significant effect on exports. Specifically,

- One expert stated most arguments asserting the tax expenditure's positive effect on exports were theoretical in nature and lacked evidence.
- Two experts stated it may be impossible to obtain data to establish such an effect.
- One expert stated that the relationship between U.S. employees abroad and exports has diminished in the past several decades, due in part to advances in information technology, which have made access to information relating to export suppliers much more widely accessible globally.

Commerce officials were not aware of any data on the relationship between the tax expenditure and exports.[49] One Commerce official stated that he believed the tax expenditure's effect on exports, if any, was small. Another Commerce official told us he was not aware of the tax expenditure being discussed during development of the National Export Initiative launched in 2010. In addition, the tax expenditure was not identified as a potential contributor towards the administration's crosscutting goal of doubling U.S. exports over 5 years.[50]

The few empirical analyses that have asserted a relationship between the tax expenditure and exports have weaknesses.[51] A 1980 study concluded that repealing the tax expenditure would lead to a decline in exports.[52] A 2005 analysis, which relied on the model results from the 1980 study to estimate the effects of the tax expenditure on the number of Americans employed abroad and on U.S. exports, drew a similar conclusion.[53] However, the model from the 1980 study has several limitations. For example, the model drew on export data from 1974, when more recent data might more accurately reflect the current relationship between the tax expenditure and exports. In addition, the model incorporated assumptions relating to the activities of Americans employed abroad in relationship to U.S. exports that may not be applicable today. For instance, while the tax expenditure is not limited to individuals working in positions that promote U.S. exports, the model assumed Americans abroad are engaged in such activities. The model also assumed non-U.S. workers were not close substitutes for American workers, though several experts we interviewed indicated that for certain overseas positions, U.S. employees have no comparative advantage, in relation to non-U.S. employees.

Moreover, even if the tax expenditure had a positive effect on exports, its effect on overall U.S. employment could depend on the current employment rate. As we noted in a recent report, Commerce[54] and trade policy researchers have asserted that in a high unemployment economy—which the United States has experienced for several years— additional exports may result in additional jobs; in contrast, in a low unemployment economy, additional exports may result in jobs shifting from one firm to another without increasing total employment.[55]

THE TAX EXPENDITURE'S NET EFFECTS ON ECONOMIC EFFICIENCY AND EQUITY ARE UNCERTAIN; SOME ALTERNATIVES COULD BETTER TARGET BENEFITS BUT WOULD ADD COMPLEXITY

Using criteria from our tax expenditure evaluation guide, we evaluated whether the tax expenditure[56]

- generates net economic benefits for society;
- is fair and equitable;
- is simple, transparent, and administrable; and
- is achieving its purpose.

The tax expenditure affects a variety of resource allocation decisions; it also affects equity in several different ways. Some of these effects are positive, while others are negative, and the magnitudes of all these effects are unknown. As a result, the tax expenditure's overall effect is uncertain. For a more detailed explanation of our assessment of these questions, see appendix IV.

Does the Tax Expenditure Generate Net Economic Benefits for Society?

A tax system reduces economic efficiency to the extent that it affects the relative prices of goods, services, or factors of production and thereby induces individuals or businesses to alter economic decisions.[57] No tax system can avoid affecting some relative prices to some extent; however, it is important to minimize these price effects unless they are intended to achieve some other beneficial social purpose. We found that the tax expenditure had effects on the following.

Choices about where to work and who to hire: The tax expenditure potentially influences the choice of some U.S. citizens between working abroad or in the United States, because it lowers the total tax that these individuals would pay on foreign earned income. These tax reductions make working abroad in lower-tax countries more attractive to U.S. citizens than doing so otherwise would be, and as a result could interfere with the efficient allocation of U.S. labor between locations.[58]

The tax expenditure also potentially influences employers' choices as to whether they should fill positions abroad with U.S. citizens or with citizens of countries that do not tax earned income on a worldwide basis. The reduction in efficiency can occur when the employer hires a less productive worker for a lower pretax salary than the U.S. citizen would demand, due to the foreign worker paying no tax to his home country. The tax expenditure counteracts these effects, but we found no evidence in the economic literature that would indicate how the magnitude of the counteracting effects compares to the negative efficiency effects we discussed earlier. Consequently, we are not able to say whether the tax expenditure improves or reduces overall economic efficiency.

Differences in costs of living: Tax relief may be justified for U.S. citizens working in countries where the costs of living are significantly higher than the United States' highest-cost locations.[59] If these taxpayers' wages are sufficiently greater than they would earn at home (reflecting higher costs of living abroad), they may be pushed into higher tax brackets. This increase in the tax bracket is another way that the tax system could reduce efficiency by affecting location and hiring decisions. Tax relief targeted to the effects of this bracket change would remove an efficiency-reducing influence on U.S. citizens' employment decisions at a lower revenue cost than the more broad tax relief provided by the tax expenditure. This same efficiency problem arises domestically with respect to cost-of-living differences within the United States. Given that the U.S. tax system does not address this problem domestically, those who have proposed a means of addressing cost-of-living differences between the United States and foreign locations note that it may only be justified if the differences are much greater internationally than domestically.

Is the Tax Expenditure Fair and Equitable?

We assessed the tax expenditure against three criteria—horizontal equity, vertical equity, and the benefits received principle—all of which require some subjective judgments. Determining who benefits from the tax expenditure, and how those benefits affect equity, can be more complicated than simply identifying which taxpayers claim the tax expenditure.[60] Given that the ultimate distribution of benefits from the FEIE is unknown, it is difficult to draw conclusions about its net effect on the equity of the tax system.[61]

Horizontal equity: Individuals with equal incomes and who are the same in terms of other characteristics deemed relevant to the ability to pay tax (such as number of dependents) should pay the same tax. Conclusions about the tax expenditure's effect on horizontal equity depend, in part, on judgments about appropriate comparison groups. For U.S. policymakers, one relevant comparison is the treatment of U.S. citizens working abroad, relative to similar U.S. citizens working in the United States. The FEIE violates this principle between these two groups unless those working abroad are deemed to be sufficiently different from their domestic counterparts due to either the potentially extreme cost-of-living differences or the differences in U.S. government services they receive.

Vertical equity: Similar to horizontal equity, individuals with higher income—or who have other characteristics that increase their ability to pay—should pay more tax than those with less ability to pay. The tax expenditure decreases vertical equity to the extent that individuals who benefit from the exclusion tend to have higher incomes than those living in the United States, unless the ultimate tax benefit falls entirely on employers. In comparison to an unlimited exclusion, the current design of the tax expenditure—specifically the dollar limit and the stacking rule[62]— moderates this negative effect.

Benefits received principle: An individual's tax payments should bear some relationship to the government benefits that individual receives. Some experts we interviewed noted that U.S. citizens working abroad for the long term receive significantly smaller benefits from U.S. government services than those living in the United States, and that this difference may justify some tax relief for the former. However, other experts said that U.S. citizens living and working abroad benefit from federal services—such as national defense, foreign affairs, income maintenance, and basic research—that produce social or humanitarian benefits that are not directly apportioned to specific individuals. For example, citizens abroad benefit from years of public investment in their education, the cost of which is typically recaptured over their lifetimes. Regardless of the benefits they receive, U.S. citizens overseas must file a U.S. tax return and pay taxes owed unless they renounce their citizenship.[63]

Is the Tax Expenditure Simple, Transparent, and Administrable?

There is widespread agreement that the U.S. worldwide tax system is complex and adds burden for taxpayers and IRS. The tax expenditure adds complexity with its eligibility rules and interactions with the FTC and other tax provisions.[64]

Transparency: Taxpayers may not fully understand their obligations under the tax expenditure. According to IRS, there is a common misconception that potentially excludable foreign earned income does not have to be reported on a U.S. tax return. IRS said that this misconception contributes to the tax gap, which is the difference between taxes owed and those paid on time. However, data do not indicate the portion of the U.S. tax gap—most recently estimated by IRS at a net $385 billion as of 2006—that is attributable to international taxpayers who fail to file U.S. tax returns, underreport their foreign income, or fail to pay U.S. taxes owed. IRS has undertaken research to study the needs of international taxpayers in helping them comply with their U.S. tax liabilities.[65]

Simplicity: According to some experts interviewed, the tax expenditure may simplify the tax compliance burdens of U.S. citizens abroad who would otherwise have to claim the FTC to avoid double taxation on foreign earned income. According to stakeholders and some experts we interviewed, the FTC can be more complex. However, this effect is uncertain for several reasons, including that we did not find evaluative studies that compare the compliance burden of the tax expenditure with the FTC.

Administrability: IRS faces challenges in administering the tax expenditure, because IRS does not have the same level of information reporting to detect noncompliance on foreign source income as it does for U.S. source income. IRS special compliance projects have found substantial noncompliance among high-risk taxpayers who are miscalculating or are ineligible to claim benefits from the tax expenditure. The Treasury Inspector

General for Tax Administration has reported on the challenges in administering the bona fide residence and physical presence tests.[66]

How Well Does the Tax Expenditure Achieve Its Purposes?

As discussed earlier, the tax expenditure's effect on foreign trade, employment, and competitiveness is uncertain. There is little evidence to indicate that the tax expenditure could have more than a limited effect on exports. Thus, it is not clear that special tax relief for the relatively small population of U.S. citizens living and working abroad positively benefits the overall well-being of the United States.

Some Alternatives to the Tax Expenditure Would Increase Efficiency and Equity, While the Effect of Others Would Depend on Details of the Reform

An assessment of the tax expenditure against criteria for good tax policy leaves room for debate regarding potential alternatives to improve the efficiency and equity, as well as to reduce complexity for taxpayers and IRS. Alternatives to the current tax expenditure range from eliminating it entirely—as proposed in several deficit reduction and tax reform proposals—to removing the maximum limit for the exclusion. We also considered alternatives to target tax relief to high cost areas and address the benefits received principle.[67]

Alternative: Eliminating the Tax Expenditure

The net effect on economic efficiency of eliminating the tax expenditure and taxing all foreign earned income is uncertain. This alternative would largely remove the influence of taxes on location decisions by U.S. citizens to work abroad, which would increase efficiency; however, at the same time, it would decrease efficiency by increasing the effect of the differential tax treatment by the United States and other countries on businesses' decisions regarding whom to hire for positions abroad. The effect of the alternative on equity is also uncertain. Elimination could be viewed as improving equity if two conditions are met: (1) there are few or no foreign locations where living costs are significantly higher than in the highest-cost locations within the United States, and (2) the additional federal taxes (in excess of the amounts offset by foreign tax credits) are broadly commensurate with the benefits that U.S. citizens working abroad receive from the U.S. government. If either of these conditions is not met, then some form of tax relief may be justified on equity grounds.

The effect on compliance burden will vary with the circumstances of the taxpayers. To the extent that the FTC form is more complicated than the FEIE form, eliminating the exclusion could increase the compliance burdens of some taxpayers who currently use the exclusion rather than the FTC. However, it would not significantly affect the compliance burden of taxpayers with earned income exceeding the exclusion limit or investment income of those who already use the FTC. IRS officials said that repealing the tax expenditure would simplify challenges associated with the FEIE bona fide residence and physical presence tests that do not apply to the FTC. Citizens working abroad in lower tax countries would face higher taxes. Those facing higher taxes or compliance costs may choose not to comply, and noncompliance could undercut the expected revenue gain from repeal.[68]

Alternative: Targeting Tax Relief for Extreme Cost of Living Differences

Economic efficiency and equity could be improved by modifying the current tax expenditure design or replacing it with an alternative tax relief that adjusts for foreign costs of living that significantly exceed those in the highest-cost U.S. locations. One approach would be to make Treasury responsible for annually determining the amount by which costs of living in foreign locations may exceed those in the highest-cost U.S. locations and for publishing adjustment factors for determining tax liabilities.[69] Whether a system of cost-of-living adjustments would be more burdensome for Treasury or taxpayers than the current tax expenditure, which already has some adjustments for higher housing expenses, depends on the degree of accuracy and completeness desired in the adjustments.[70] The federal revenue change would depend on the cost of tax reductions targeted to citizens working in higher-cost foreign areas, instead of the current preferential treatment for all citizens working abroad, and—depending on policy priorities and preferences—the redesign could aim for the same or a lower overall cost to the federal government.

Alternative: Targeting Tax Relief Based on Benefits Received and Obligations as Citizens

It would be difficult to design an alternative to the tax expenditure that better targeted tax relief based on benefits received. The tax expenditure itself is not designed specifically to address the benefits received principle, and the federal income tax in general is not based on the benefits received principle. Indeed, it would be very difficult to incorporate the principle in a tax that funds such a broad array of functions, many of which provide broad social benefits. Moreover, the values of these benefits are not easily allocable to specific individuals. Any attempt to determine a fair reduction in federal tax obligations of U.S. citizens living abroad—relative to similar citizens living in the United States—would involve a considerable amount of value judgment. Depending on policy priorities and preferences, any redesign targeted for reduced benefits received by citizens working overseas could aim for the same or a lower overall cost to the federal government. A revision deemed to result in a more equitable distribution of the tax burden would not necessarily have negative consequences for economic efficiency. The effects of the revision on simplicity and administrability would largely depend on the extent to which it is designed to account for the characteristics of individual taxpayers. One possible change in the current tax expenditure design would be to increase the time abroad required for eligibility. This would target tax relief to those abroad for longer periods.[71]

Alternative: Uncapping the Exclusion

Removing the maximum limit on the exclusion—that is, uncapping the tax expenditure—and excluding all foreign earned income from taxation would have multiple counteracting effects on employment decisions. These effects would be opposite to those that would result from eliminating the tax expenditure. In this case, inefficiency due to tax effects on location decisions would increase while inefficiency due to the tax effects on hiring would decrease. Once again, because the relative magnitudes of the counteracting effects are indeterminable, the net effect on overall economic efficiency would be uncertain. The effect on equity will depend on value judgments. Uncapping the tax expenditure could be viewed as reducing both horizontal and vertical equity because it would reduce the federal tax liabilities of some high-income U.S. citizens working in countries with effective rates of income tax below that of the United States, regardless of the cost of living differences. On the other hand, it would increase equity if U.S. citizens working abroad are viewed as receiving no benefits for which they should pay federal taxes. To the extent that the exclusion is easier to use than the FTC, uncapping the exclusion could simplify compliance burdens for citizens abroad with only earned income, although they would still have to file a U.S. tax return to claim the tax benefit. However, uncapping the exclusion could compound the challenge that IRS has in administering the tax expenditure, given the misconception that those with excluded income do not have to file and report income to IRS. According to some experts we interviewed, uncapping the exclusion could create incentives for higher-income professionals to move abroad to deliver their services and to shift some investment income to be paid as earned income. It would also reduce federal tax revenue, and any perceived unfairness could erode voluntary compliance for domestic taxpayers. Experiences of other countries that do not tax foreign earned income may be useful in adopting tax rules and compliance practices to prevent or limit income shifting to lower tax countries.[72]

Uncapping the exclusion and not taxing any foreign earned income would be consistent with broader proposals to change the current U.S. worldwide system of taxation into a territorial or source based income tax system. One proposal to move from "citizen-based" to "resident-based" taxation would exclude all foreign income for individuals living abroad; this could make the tax expenditure unnecessary.[73] Such an approach would impose a departure tax for citizens working abroad who reside in a foreign country for a minimum period of time.[74] Some proposals have implications not only for U.S. individual income tax filing, but also for information reporting about foreign financial accounts and assets that are beyond the scope of this report.[75] The larger debate about broader changes to the U.S. international tax system focuses chiefly on the taxation of corporate income, and such reforms may have implications for the tax treatment of the wage income of U.S. citizens working abroad; however, they are beyond the scope of this report.

Concluding Observations

The design of the tax expenditure has shifted over time as policymakers have sought to balance the costs of special tax relief to cover higher costs of living overseas with benefits for individuals seeking employment overseas and potentially, benefits for U.S. exports. Currently, the federal government is forgoing billions in federal tax revenue for a small but growing population of U.S. citizens working abroad that claim section 911 tax benefits. Yet, there is little evidence that the tax expenditure has a significant effect on export promotion.

It is clear that the current tax expenditure, or any option to increase the exclusion limit, does not target precisely the two potential conditions that might justify continuing tax relief for some U.S. citizens living and working abroad. First, potentially negative effects on efficiency and equity could arise if the cost of living in foreign locations significantly exceeds that of the highest-cost locations in the United States. Determining whether extreme cost of living differences justify special tax relief, and how to tailor the alternative relief is—to some extent—an empirical question. Second, a possible inequity could arise if U.S. citizens working abroad receive a reduced level of U.S. government benefits compared to what they would receive if they were living in the United States. Considering special tax relief based on benefits received by citizens abroad requires broader value judgments about the extent to which U.S. citizens should contribute to government services from which they may receive no direct private benefit. In addition, any alternative to better target special tax relief must balance added complexity for taxpayers and IRS, as well as revenue implications for the federal government.

Eliminating any special tax relief could reduce the employment of U.S. citizens in some international job markets and might lead to a small reduction in U.S. businesses' foreign activities. However, there is no clear evidence that such effects would have negative consequences for the overall well being of the U.S. population.

Agency Comments and Our Methodology

We provided a draft of this report to the Secretary of the Treasury, Commissioner of Internal Revenue, and the Secretary of Commerce for and Our Evaluation comment. Treasury and IRS provided technical comments, which we incorporated as appropriate. Commerce said it had no comments.

James R. McTigue, Jr.
Director, Tax Issues
Strategic Issues

Appendix I. Objectives, Scope, and Methodology

You asked us to examine section 911—the foreign earned income exclusion (FEIE) as well as an exclusion or deduction for foreign housing costs. Specifically, this report (1) describes the number and types of taxpayers using the tax expenditure, and analyzes how the tax expenditure may interact with other provisions of the tax code, such as the foreign tax credit; (2)

describes what is known about how the tax expenditure may affect business decisions about the employment of U.S. workers abroad, and U.S. exports; and (3) evaluates the potential advantages and disadvantages of modifying or removing the tax expenditure.

To describe the number and types of taxpayers using the FEIE, we reviewed Internal Revenue Service (IRS) forms and publications. We did not try to count the population of U.S. citizens working abroad. We also analyzed data from the IRS's Statistics of Income (SOI) *Individual Income Tax Returns 2011 publication*, and from data obtained from SOI on Form 2555, Foreign Earned Income and Form 2555-EZ, Foreign Earned Income Exclusion, for tax year 2011(the most recent year available). These SOI samples were based on returns as filed, and did not reflect IRS audit results or any net operating loss carrybacks from future years. Each Form 2555/EZ is treated as a separate return which, in the case of joint returns, may be composed of more than one taxpayer. The SOI data in this report is based on SOI's probability sample of unaudited individual income tax returns—Forms 1040, 1040A, and 1040EZ (including electronic returns) filed by U.S. citizens and residents[76]—and thus is subject to some imprecision owing to sampling variability. Using SOI's summaries of sampling weights and coefficient of variations, we estimated sampling errors for our estimates. However, SOI did not provide coefficient of variations for all of the data we obtained. As a result, when possible, estimates were obtained using the coefficients of variations of other items. Some data could not be reported and some had to be aggregated. Unless otherwise noted, all percentage estimates based on the SOI have 95 percent confidence intervals. Caution should be used when comparing estimates because not all differences between estimates are statistically significant.

SOI is a data set widely used for research purposes. SOI data are not available to the public except in aggregate form via published tables. These data tables are publicly available either in printed form or on the IRS website (http://www.irs.gov). IRS performs a number of quality control steps to verify the internal consistency of SOI sample data. For example, it performs computerized tests to verify the relationships between values on the returns selected as part of the SOI sample, and manually edits data items to correct for problems, such as missing items. To assess the reliability of the data we analyzed, we reviewed IRS documentation and interviewed agency officials familiar with the data. We concluded that the data were sufficiently reliable for the purposes of this report.

To determine how the tax expenditure may interact with other provisions of the tax code, we reviewed the Internal Revenue Code (IRC) for references to section 911. We also reviewed section 911 for references to other provisions of the U.S. Code, including the IRC. Although we identified provisions that reference section 911, not all provisions may have been identified. We did not attempt to identify provisions that refer to other provisions which refer to section 911. Through interviews and review of IRS and other materials, we identified some provisions of law that, while not referencing section 911 or referenced in section 911, may interact in some way with section 911; however, not all such provisions may have been identified. As procedural requirements, information reporting about foreign financial accounts and offshore assets—such as under the Foreign Account Tax Compliance Act or the Report of Foreign Bank and Financial Accounts—affects U.S. citizens living and working abroad but is beyond the scope of this report, which is examining section 911. To analyze how the tax expenditure affects eligibility for other tax provisions, we reviewed IRS publications, guidance, and tax advisor literature. We did not try to quantify the number and types of taxpayers using the tax expenditure that are specifically affected by the interactions.

To determine what is known about how the tax expenditure may affect business decisions about the employment of U.S. workers abroad, and U.S. exports, we reviewed related literature and available information, including government reports, academic literature, and surveys. In particular, we identified literature by conducting searches of academic literature databases, such as ProQuest, Econlit, and ABI/INFORM; searches of our prior work and work from the Congressional Budget Office (CBO), Congressional Research Service (CRS), Joint Committee on Taxation (JCT), Department of Treasury (Treasury), and Internal Revenue Service (IRS); or searches of bibliographies from literature already identified, such as the tax expenditure compendium prepared by the Congressional Research Service.[77] Although there is an extensive literature on the United States' taxation of worldwide income, much of that literature is focused on the taxation of corporations.[78] The literature related to the FEIE is more limited in volume. Prior GAO and CRS in-depth reports are more than 30 years old.[79] Other studies and articles were derived from or sponsored by industry groups or other organizations that may benefit from adjustments to laws and regulations governing the FEIE. Subsequently, we interviewed a selection of agency officials, experts, and stakeholder organizations and entities, and asked all interviewees for their suggestions on available literature and data concerning the FEIE to supplement our own literature review. (We define stakeholders as individuals or groups who may offer a valuable perspective on how the tax expenditure may affect business decisions concerning the employment of U.S. workers abroad, and exports, but who may also have a vested interest in the issue.) We interviewed Department of Commerce officials. We also identified a pool of 33 experts, whom we selected based on various factors including their affiliation with leading higher education or research institutions and their publication or research experience associated with the FEIE or related topics. These experts included economists, attorneys, and business professors, among others. One consideration in the selection process was to talk with experts with different areas of expertise among the issues of international taxation, international business strategy, trade, or U.S. labor. Another consideration was to talk with experts whose overall views on the FEIE varied from one another. While we were able to include some experts with a range of views based on their published work, most that we identified had not published articles specifically on the FEIE. Therefore, we did not know their overall opinions of FEIE in advance of our interview.

We interviewed nine of these experts who we determined provided the range of background and experiences that we were seeking. However, the views and opinions of the experts we interviewed may not represent those of all the experts in this area. We interviewed the following experts:

- Reuven Avi-Yonah, Professor of Law, University of Michigan
- Jamie Bonache, Professor of Organization Studies, Carlos III University of Madrid
- Kimberly Clausing, Professor of Economics, Reed College
- Gary Hufbauer, Senior Fellow, Peterson Institute for International Economics
- Michael Kirsch, Professor of Law, University of Notre Dame
- Daniel Mitchell, Senior Fellow, Cato Institute
- John Mutti, Professor of Economics, Grinnell College
- Maury Peiperl, Professor of Leadership and Strategic Change, IMD Business School
- Eric Toder, Institute Fellow, Urban Institute

In addition, we interviewed representatives from nine stakeholder organizations that represent the interests of relevant entities, such as U.S. citizens working overseas and U.S. businesses. These organizations represent businesses in different geographical regions, and of different sizes. This sample of stakeholder perspectives covers a range of views, but is not generalizable to all stakeholders. In particular, we interviewed representatives from the following organizations:

- American Citizens Abroad, Inc.
- Association of Americans Resident Overseas
- Business Roundtable
- Middle East Council of American Chambers of Commerce
- National Foreign Trade Council
- National Small Business Association
- KPMG LLP
- PricewaterhouseCoopers LLP
- U.S. Chamber of Commerce, Asia

We used our review of the literature and available information described above to inform our development of sets of questions and discussion topics for the interviewees. Our discussion topics and questions for experts and stakeholders covered different areas such as the tax expenditure's costs, benefits, and other characteristics; its relationship to U.S. workers and companies; and its relationship to exports. We analyzed all expert and stakeholder responses, and generally reported on areas where interviewees provided information that was most relevant to our final reporting objectives. In our reporting of expert and stakeholder views, we refer to "most" experts or stakeholders as representing 7 or more; "about half" as representing 4 to 6; and "several" or "some" as representing 2 or 3. While we are presenting approximate proportions of all experts and stakeholders, not every expert and stakeholders directly addressed each issue.

To identify and analyze alternative policy options, we reviewed the same literature described above to determine what is known about the advantages and disadvantages of modifying the foreign earned income exclusion. We also obtained the views of the nine experts and nine stakeholders we interviewed on the advantages and disadvantages of modifying the tax expenditure.

Our discussion topics and questions for experts and stakeholders covered a range of possible options for modifying the tax expenditure, as shown in table 7. We focused our analysis on the most common options discussed in the literature and by those we interviewed—eliminating the tax expenditure with taxing all foreign earned income and uncapping the exclusion with no taxation of foreign earned income. We also examined options that could address two arguments that may justify providing some tax relief: (1) targeting extreme costs of living to improve efficiency, and (2) adjusting taxes to reflect lower benefits to improve equity.

Table 7. Various Possible Options to Modify the Design of the Current Exclusion

Repeal the FEIE, foreign housing exclusion, or both, and tax all foreign earned income.
Reduce the maximum exclusion, housing cost amount, or both.
Increase the maximum exclusion, housing cost amount, or both.
Restrict eligibility, for example, by lengthening the required time of the bona fide residence test and the physical presence test for U.S. citizens and U.S. resident aliens living in a foreign country or by targeting employees who work in specific industries.
Expand eligibility, for example, by shortening the required time of the bona fide residence test and the physical presence test for U.S. citizens and U.S. resident aliens living in a foreign country or by extending eligibility to maritime and aviation workers who do not meet the current physical presence test.
Change the way the exclusion and housing cost limits are computed. The foreign earned income exclusion is currently indexed for inflation using the Consumer Price Index, and housing cost limits are computed by geography. One possibility would be to change how the tax expenditure is indexed for the cost of living.
Change the interactions with other tax provisions. Currently, claiming the tax expenditure affects taxpayer eligibility for other tax provisions with income thresholds, such as individual retirement accounts and the earned income tax credit. Since 2006, a stacking rule or provision requires that marginal tax rates apply to earnings beyond the limits of the tax expenditure, as if the tax expenditure had not been claimed. One way to change the interaction and stacking order would be to convert the exclusion to a credit.
Replace the exclusion with an overseas employment tax credit targeted to employees of selected industries. For example, Canadians can claim an overseas employment tax credit if they are a resident or deemed resident of Canada at any time in the year and have income from certain kinds of work—such as oil and gas exploration, construction, engineering, and work under contract with the United Nations, among others—performed in another country.
Uncap the exclusion and exclude all foreign earned income from taxation.
Impose an exit fee on U.S. citizens and U.S. resident aliens living in a foreign country. Usually part of broader tax reform, this option would exclude all foreign income for eligible individuals living overseas.

Source: GAO analysis.

We used the tax expenditure evaluation guide we developed to evaluate the performance of the foreign earned income exclusion and possibleoptions.[80] This report focuses on the guide's criteria for evaluating whether the tax expenditure is good tax policy and meets its purpose, namely,

- Does the tax expenditure generate net economic benefits for society?
- Is the tax expenditure fair and equitable?
- Is the tax expenditure simple, transparent, and administrable?
- How well does the tax expenditure achieve its purpose?

The tax policy criteria may sometimes conflict with one another and some are subjective. As a result, there are likely trade-offs between the criteria when evaluating a particular tax expenditure. We also considered the consequences for the federal budget of the tax expenditure and possible options. We analyzed Treasury's tax expenditure estimates from 1986 to2014, and reviewed available JCT estimates and interviewed JCT staff about the revenue effects of modifying the tax expenditure.

APPENDIX II. PROVISIONS THAT INTERACT WITH SECTION 911

There are different types of tax provisions that interact with section 911. Some tax provisions apply to Americans working abroad. Other tax provisions use the Foreign Earned Income Exclusion (FEIE) to determine the taxpayer's tax rate and the applicability for other tax provisions. There are also tax provisions that provide definitions, some of which are relevant in interpreting section 911. The tables below describe provisions that interact with section 911.

Table 8 lists select tax provisions and tax treaties which affect income tax treatment for U.S. taxpayers with income from foreign sources.

Table 9 lists other tax provisions which specifically reference section 911. In general, these provisions require calculating the taxpayer's income for a specific purpose, such as for determining eligibility for a credit or deduction, and require some or all of the exclusions or deductions allowed under section 911 to be included in the calculation. Most of the provisions listed in table 9 would not be affected by amendments to section 911, as changing the allowable exclusion or deduction under section 911 would not affect the net resulting calculation of income for purposes of most of these provisions.

Table 8. Selected Provisions Affecting Income Tax Treatments for Americans Working Abroad

Description of provision	Description of provision	Interaction with section 911
Foreign tax credit 26 U.S.C § 901	The foreign tax credit is intended to relieve double taxation when foreign income is taxed by both the United States and the foreign country. Only foreign income taxes (including war taxes and excess profits taxes) paid or accrued to any foreign country or any possession of the United States can be claimed for the foreign tax credit. If the foreign tax rate is higher than the U.S. rate, there will be no U.S. tax on the foreign income. If the foreign tax rate is lower than the U.S. rate, U.S. tax on the foreign income will be limited to the difference between the rates. Taxpayers can choose to claim the foreign tax credit on IRS Form 1116 or as an itemized deduction on the Form 1040 schedule A.	Taxpayers who choose to claim the foreign earned income exclusion cannot take a foreign tax credit or deduction for foreign taxes on the income excluded. There is no double taxation because the excluded income is not subject to U.S income tax.
Exemption for certain federal employee allowances 26 U.S.C § 912.	Special allowances—cost of living, housing, travel, and education—for federal civilian employees who work abroad are excluded for federal income taxes. Federal employees are generally exempt from foreign taxes.	Federal employees are not eligible for the foreign earned income or housing exclusion.

Table 8. (Continued)

Description of provision	Description of provision	Interaction with section 911
Tax treaties[a]	The United States has tax treaties with other countries that allow residents of those countries, including U.S. citizens and residents, to enjoy certain benefits, such as reduced rates of withholding and exemption from tax on certain items of income. Tax treaties may provide benefits to Americans working abroad, specifically: • compensation from short-term business trips may be excluded from taxation in the foreign country, and • pay for teachers, professors, students, trainees, and apprentices may be excluded from taxation in the foreign country.	Treaty benefits may also be available for U.S. citizens working abroad with U.S. tax home who do not meet the residency requirements for the foreign earned income and housing exclusion.
Expatriation tax 26 U.S.C § 877 and 877A	Expatriation tax provisions apply to U.S. citizens who have relinquished their citizenship and to long-term residents who have ceased to be lawful permanent residents. The rules that apply are based on the date of expatriation, as described in IRS Publication 519—U.S. Tax Guide for Aliens.	An expatriate who is considered a "covered expatriate" and whose expatriation date is after June 16, 2008 is generally subject to tax—on the net unrealized gain in his or her property as if the property had been sold for its fair market value on the day before the expatriation date. An expatriate may avoid being considered a "covered expatriate" if the section 911 exclusion reduces the expatriate's U.S. income tax liability below a certain threshold for the five years prior to expatriation.

Source: GAO analysis of the United States Code.

[a] Taxpayers using the foreign tax credit for income taxes can claim only taxes paid. The qualified foreign tax is the amount figured using the lower treaty rate and not the amount actually paid, because the excess tax is refundable.

Table 9. Foreign Earned Income Excluded Is Used to Determine Tax Rates and Applicability for Other Tax Provisions

Other provision and citation to reference in provision to section 911	Description of provision	Interaction with section 911
Requirement to file a U.S. income tax return 26 U.S.C § 6012(c)	Income, filing status, and age generally determine whether a taxpayer must file an income tax return. For 2013, a single taxpayer under age 65 with worldwide income of $10,000 must file a U.S. tax return.	Foreign earned income and foreign housing amounts that can be excluded under section 911 are included in determining whether a taxpayer's income is high enough to trigger the requirement to file a tax return.
Figuring tax on income not excluded 26 U.S.C § 1[a]	Worldwide income of U.S. citizens or resident aliens is generally subject to U.S. income tax regardless of where they are living. The marginal rate of tax increases for higher amounts of income.	Taxpayers claiming the foreign earned income exclusion, the housing exclusion, or both, must compute the tax on their nonexcluded income using the tax rates that would have applied had they not claimed the exclusions.
Alternative minimum tax[a] 26 U.S.C § 5581	The alternative minimum tax is a separate income tax calculation intended to ensure that higher-income taxpayers pay at least a minimum tax. Individuals with high levels of exemptions, deductions, and credits relative to income may be subject to the alternative minimum tax.	Taxpayers claiming the foreign earned income exclusion, the housing exclusion, or both, must compute the alternative minimum tax on their nonexcluded income using the tax rates that would have applied had they not claimed the exclusions.

Table 9. (Continued)

Other provision and citation to reference in provision to section 911	Description of provision	Interaction with section 911
Earned income credit[b] 26 U.S.C § 32(c)(1)(C)	The earned income tax credit is a refundable credit available to low income workers. Qualifying working taxpayers may receive a refund greater than the amount of income tax they paid for the year.	Taxpayers that claim the foreign earned income exclusion cannot also claim the earned income credit.
Child tax credit 26 U.S.C. §24(b)(1)	The child tax credit is a credit that can reduce tax by as much as $1,000 for each qualifying child under age 17. The additional child tax credit is refundable for taxpayers that owe no taxes. The amount of the credit is phased-out at higher levels of income.	Foreign earned income and foreign housing amounts that can be excluded under section 911 are included in determining income for purposes of the phase-out.
Adoption Credit 26 U.S.C. §23(b)(2)(B)	A tax credit of up to $12,970 is allowed for qualified expenses paid to adopt an eligible child, including a child with special needs. The amount of the credit is phased-out at higher levels of income.	Foreign earned income and foreign housing amounts, or both, that can be excluded under section 911 are included in determining income for purposes of the phase-out.
Adoption Exclusion 26 U.S.C. §137(b)(3)	A taxpayer may be able to exclude from income amounts paid or expenses incurred by their employer for qualified adoption expenses in connection with adopting a child. The maximum amount of the exclusion is phased-out at higher levels of income.	Foreign earned income and foreign housing amounts that can be excluded under section 911 are included in determining income for purposes of the phase-out.

Other provision and citation to reference in provision to section 911	Description of provision	Interaction with section 911
Hope Scholarship Credit, Lifetime Learning Credit, and American Opportunity Credit 26 U.S.C. § 25A(d)(3)	These tax credits are available to taxpayers who pay expenses for higher (postsecondary) education expenses. For 2009 to 2017, a special type of Hope Scholarship Credit (with higher minimums and called the American Opportunities Credit) is available. The maximum amount of the credits is phased-out at higher levels of income.	Foreign earned income and foreign housing amounts that can be excluded under section 911 are included in determining income for purposes of the phase-out.
Student Loan Interest Deduction 26 U.S.C. § 221(b)(2)(C)	Generally, personal interest, other than certain mortgage interest, is not deductible. This special deduction is allowed for paying interest on a student loan (also known as an education loan) used for higher education. The maximum allowable deduction is phased-out at higher income levels.	Foreign earned income and foreign housing amounts that can be excluded under section 911 are included in determining income for purposes of the phase-out.
Tuition and Fees Deduction 26 U.S.C. § 222(b)(2)(C)	This deduction is allowed for qualified higher education expenses paid during the year for the taxpayer, spouse, or dependents. The maximum allowable deduction for taxpayers decreases at higher levels of income.	Foreign earned income and foreign housing amounts that can be excluded under section 911 are included in calculating the level of income used to determine the maximum deduction.
Coverdell Education Savings Account (ESA) 26 U.S.C. § 530(c)(2)	A Coverdell ESA is a tax-preferred account created or organized in the United States only for the purpose	Foreign earned income and foreign housing amounts that can be excluded under section 911 are included in

Table 9. (Continued)

Other provision and citation to reference in provision to section 911	Description of provision	Interaction with section 911
	of paying qualified education expenses. The total annual contribution limit starts at $2,000 per beneficiary (through age 17 unless he or she is a special needs beneficiary) and is phased-out at higher levels of income. Distributions used to pay qualified education expenses are tax-exempt.	determining income for purposes of the phase-out.
Interest from U.S. savings bonds used to pay higher education expenses 26 U.S.C. § 135(c)(4)	All or part of the interest received on the redemption of qualified U.S. savings bonds used to pay qualified higher educational expenses during the same year is excluded from income. The maximum allowable exclusion is phased-out at higher income levels.	Foreign earned income and foreign housing amounts that can be excluded under section 911 are included in determining income for purposes of the phase-out.
Deduction phase-out for individual retirement account contributions 26 U.S.C. § 219(g)(3)	If individuals or their spouses actively participate in certain other retirement arrangements during a year, their deductions for contributions to traditional IRAs are subject to a phase-out range based on income.	Foreign earned income and foreign housing amounts that can be excluded under section 911 are included in determining income for purposes of the phase-out.
Saver's credit 26 U.S.C. § 25B(e)	The amount of the saver's credit is equal to the applicable percentage of the individual's qualified retirement savings	Foreign earned income and foreign housing amounts that can be excluded under section 911 are included in determining income for

Other provision and citation to reference in provision to section 911	Description of provision	Interaction with section 911
	contributions. The maximum possible credit is $1,000. The higher the income of the taxpayer, the lower the applicable percentage is.	purposes of applicable percentage.
Contribution phase-out for Roth individual retirement account contributions 26 U.S.C. § 408A(c)(3)(B)(i)	Taxpayers may make contributions to Roth individual retirement accounts up to an annual contribution limit. There is no deduction for contributions, but earnings of the account are not taxed when earned and are excluded from income when distributed. Otherwise allowable contributions are subject to a phase-out range based on income.	Foreign earned income and foreign housing amounts that can be excluded under section 911 are included in determining income for purposes of the phase-out.
Annuities 26 U.S.C. § 72(f)	Annuity payments may be fully or partially taxable depending in part on the tax treatment of the initial contributions. When an employer contributes to an employee's annuity, these contributions do not count towards the amount of the exclusion unless they were included in the employee's income when made.	If contributions to an annuity by an employer would not be includible in the income of the employee at the time they were made because of section 911, the contributions are not counted towards the exclusion.
Refundable credit for coverage under a qualified health plan	In general, taxpayers with household income between 100 and 400 percent of the national poverty line are allowed a refundable tax	Foreign earned income and foreign housing amounts that can be excluded under section 911 are included in determining household income.

Table 9. (Continued)

Other provision and citation to reference in provision to section 911	Description of provision	Interaction with section 911
26 U.S.C. § 36B(d)(2)(B)	credit for coverage under a qualified health plan.	
Unearned Income Medicare Contribution 26 U.S.C. § 1411(d)(1)	Individuals with adjusted gross income—as modified under this section—above certain threshold amounts and with net investment income owe a tax equal to the lesser of 3.8 percent of that net investment income or 3.8 percent of the excess of the individual's modified adjusted gross income over the applicable threshold amount.	Foreign earned income excluded under section 911(a)(1) (if any) is included in determining the amount of income that is compared against the applicable threshold amount in applying this section, but only to the extent the excluded income exceeds the amount of any deductions (taken into account in computing adjusted gross income) or exclusions disallowed under section 911(d)(6) with respect to the amounts excluded from gross income under 911(a)(1).
Penalty under the requirement to maintain minimum essential coverage 26 U.S.C. § 5000A(c)(4)(C)	Individuals who do not maintain minimum essential healthcare insurance coverage are subject to a penalty. The penalty amount is the greater of a flat dollar amount or a percentage of income. Individuals with income below certain thresholds are not subject the penalty.	Foreign earned income and foreign housing amounts that can be excluded under section 911 are included in determining income for purposes of the penalty and thresholds.
Self-Employed Health Insurance Deduction 26 U.S.C. § 162(l)	In general, self-employed individuals are allowed to deduct the cost of health insurance. The deduction	Foreign earned income and foreign housing amounts that can be excluded under section 911 are included in

Other provision and citation to reference in provision to section 911	Description of provision	Interaction with section 911
	cannot exceed the taxpayer's earned income derived from the trade or business in which the taxpayer is self-employed.	determining the amount of earned income for purpose of the allowable deduction for self-employed health insurance.
Social security and tier 1 railroad retirement benefits 26 U.S.C § 86(b)(2)	A percentage of social security and certain railroad retirement benefits paid to individuals with incomes above certain thresholds is considered income and is taxed accordingly. Above one set of income thresholds, 85 percent of the benefits are considered income. Above a lower set of thresholds, 50 percent of the benefits are considered income. Individuals with income below an even lower set of thresholds are not taxed on these benefits.	Foreign earned income and foreign housing amounts that can be excluded under section 911 are included in determining income for purposes of the thresholds.
Includible compensation for purposes of taxation of employee annuities 26 USC § 403(b)(3)	Annuity contracts purchased by a tax exempt non-profit or public school for certain employees are excluded from the income of the employee until a distribution is made. The amounts an employer can contribute to the employee's annuity are limited, in part, by the amount of compensation received by the employee from the employer.	Foreign earned income and foreign housing amounts that can be excluded under section 911 are included in determining the amount of compensation received by the employee from the employer.

Table 9. (Continued)

Other provision and citation to reference in provision to section 911	Description of provision	Interaction with section 911
Limitation on benefits under qualified defined benefit plans 26 USC § 415(b)(3)	Trusts which form part of a defined benefit pension plan of an employer and meet certain requirements are considered qualified trusts and provide certain tax benefits. A trust is not a qualified trust if it is a defined benefit plan and provides benefits in excess of a certain limitation. Benefits exceed the limitation if, on an annual basis, they are greater than the lesser of $160,000 (subject to cost-of-living adjustments) or 100 percent of the participant's average compensation for high 3 years.	For a self-employed individual, foreign earned income and foreign housing amounts that can be excluded under section 911 are included in determining average compensation for high 3 years.
Qualified individual present in foreign country or countries, applicability of exclusion from gross income provided by this section for self-employment tax purposes 26 U.S.C § 1402(a)(8), (11)	Self-employed individuals owe a tax on their self-employment income, consisting of an old-age, survivors, and disability insurance tax and a hospital insurance tax. In general, an individual's self-employment income is the net earnings from self-employment subject to certain limitations.	Foreign earned income that can be excluded under section 911(a)(1) is included in determining net earnings from self-employment. Additionally, net earnings from self-employment for ministers are determined without regard to section 911.

Source: GAO analysis of the United States Code.

[a] These provisions do not include a reference to section 911. Subsection (f)(1) of section 911 sets forth these interactions.

[b] Unlike the other entries in this table, amendments to section 911 could potentially affect the earned income credit. For instance, if the foreign earned income exclusion was eliminated, some taxpayers who had been taking the foreign earned income exclusion might be newly eligible for the earned income credit.

Table 10 lists provisions, including two non-tax statutes which provide definitions or other context relevant for interpreting section 911.

Table 11 lists tax provisions which incorporate by reference a definition established in section 911, such as “earned income” and “tax home”.

Table 10. Provisions Which Provide Definitions Relevant in Interpreting Section 911

Other provision and citation	Description of other provision	Interaction with section 911
Social security and tier 1 railroad retirement benefits 26 U.S.C § 86(f)(4)	A percentage of social security and certain railroad retirement benefits paid to individuals with incomes above certain thresholds is considered income and is taxed accordingly. In addition, this provision provides that for purposes of section 911, any social security benefit shall be treated as an amount received as a pension or annuity.	Under section 911, amounts received by an individual as a pension or annuity are not considered foreign earned income.
Taxability of beneficiary of employees’ trust 26 U.S.C § 402(b)	Under section 402(b) benefits under a non-tax exempt employees’ trust may be included in the gross income of the employees before they are actually distributed. The provision specifies the amount and timing of this income.	Under section 911, amounts included in gross income because of section 402(b) are not considered foreign earned income.
Taxation of employee annuities 26 U.S.C § 403(c)	In general, if an employer purchases an annuity contract for an employee and that annuity meets certain requirements, the employee	Under section 911, amounts included in gross income because of section 403(c) are not considered foreign earned income.

Table 10. (Continued)

Other provision and citation	Description of other provision	Interaction with section 911
	will be taxed on amounts distributed from the annuity to the employee in the year the distributions are made. Under section 403(c), premiums paid by an employer for an annuity contract which fails to meet these requirements are to be included in the gross income of an employee and are governed by different timing rules.	
Trade or business expenses 26 U.S.C § 162(a)(2)	Taxpayers are allowed to deduct ordinary and necessary business expenses including traveling expenses while away from home in the pursuit of a trade or business. In interpreting "while away from home", the courts have developed a body of case law defining a taxpayer's "tax home". In general, a person's tax home for determining deductible traveling expenses is the vicinity of his or her principle place of business and not where his or her personal residence is located.	For purposes of section 911, an individual's "tax home" is the home from which travel is a deductible business expense under section 162, with the caveat that an individual's tax home is not considered to be in a foreign country for purposes of section 911 for any period for which his or her abode is within the United States. To be eligible for an exclusion under section 911, a taxpayer's tax home must be in a foreign country, among other requirements.
Cost of living adjustment 26 U.S.C § 1(f)(3)	The IRC requires certain dollar amounts to be adjusted annually for inflation according to a statutory formula based on the difference between the consumer price index in a	For taxable years beginning after 2005, the maximum foreign earned income exclusion amount is adjusted for inflation according to the calculation set forth in section 1(f)(3)

Other provision and citation	Description of other provision	Interaction with section 911
	price index for a reference given year and the consumer year. This formula is set forth in section 1(f)(3).	with 2004 as the reference year.
Mortgage Interest 26 U.S.C § 163	In general, under section 163, individuals can deduct business or investment interest, but not personal interest unless it is qualified residence interest on a home mortgage loan.	Housing expenses for purposes of section 911 do not include interest deductible under section 163.
Property Tax 26 U.S.C § 164	In general, individuals can deduct certain taxes, including state, local, and foreign real property taxes, state and local personal property taxes, and state, local, and foreign income taxes.	Housing expenses for purposes of section 911 do not include taxes deductible under section 164.
Deduction of taxes, interest, and business depreciation by cooperative housing corporation tenant-stockholder 26 U.S.C § 216(a)	Under section 216(a) a tenant-stockholder can deduct amounts paid or accrued to a cooperative housing corporation to the extent such payments represent the tenant-shareholder's proportional share of deductible real estate taxes or deductible interest.	Housing expenses for purposes of section 911 do not include amounts deductible under section 216(a).
Gain from dispositions of certain depreciable realty 26 USC § 1250	In general, taxpayers can deduct depreciation on certain real property that is more than the depreciation figured using the straight line method. This excess depreciation is referred to as additional depreciation. Gain on the disposition of real property with the additional depreciation is	When determining the amount of tax owed, unrecaptured section 1250 gains are determined after increasing the amount by any capital gain excess.

Table 10. (Continued)

Other provision and citation	Description of other provision	Interaction with section 911
	treated as ordinary income to the extent of the additional depreciation and is taxed at a maximum 25 percent rate.	
Wages defined for income tax withholding provisions in relation to exclusion from gross income under this section 26 U.S.C § 3401(a)(8)	Generally, for income tax withholding purposes, wages mean all remuneration for services performed by an employee for an employer.	For income tax withholding purposes, wages do not include services for an employer if, at the time of the payment of such remuneration, it is reasonable to believe that such remuneration will be excluded from gross income under section 911.
Place where persons claiming benefits of this section file returns 26 U.S.C § 6091	In general, individuals file tax returns in the internal revenue district of their legal residence of principle place of business or at a service center serving that internal revenue district as the Secretary by regulation may designate.	Persons claiming exclusions or deductions under section 911 file tax returns where designated by regulations, which direct taxpayers to file in accordance with the applicable Forms and Instructions.
Trading With the Enemy Act 50 U.S.C. App. §§ 1–44	Restricts trade with countries hostile to the United States. The act also authorizes the use of economic sanctions against foreign nations, citizens and nationals of foreign countries, or other persons aiding a foreign country.	If travel or any transaction in connection with such travel with respect to any foreign country is regulated under the Trading with the Enemy Act, then income from that country is not considered foreign earned income, and, therefore, not excludable. Further expenses for housing in that country or for a spouse or dependents in another country while the taxpayer is in the regulated country are not considered housing expenses, and, therefore

Other provision and citation	Description of other provision	Interaction with section 911
		are not excludable or deductible. Individuals in a regulated country are not considered bona fide residents of that country or present in that country.
International Emergency Economic Powers Act (50 U.S.C. 1701 et seq.),	Authorizes the President to regulate commerce after declaring a national emergency in response to any unusual and extraordinary threat to the United States which has a foreign source. It gives the President broad authority over financial transactions and property in which any foreign country, any citizen or national of a foreign country, or any other person aiding the foreign country, has any interest, provided that the president first declares a national emergency under the act.	If travel or any transaction in connection with such travel with respect to any foreign country is regulated under the Trading with the Enemy Act, then income from that country is not considered foreign earned income, and, therefore, not excludable. Further expenses for housing in that country or for a spouse or dependents in another country while the taxpayer is in the regulated country are not considered housing expenses, and, therefore are not excludable or deductible. Individuals in a regulated country are not considered bona fide residents of that country or present in that country.

Source: GAO analysis of the United States Code.

Table 11. Section 911 Definition Is Used in Defining Earned Income or Tax Home

Description of provision	Wording of provision	Interaction with section 911
Certain unearned income of children taxed as if parent's income	For certain children, unearned income over $2,000 is taxed at the parent's rate if the parent's rate is higher than the child's.	This provision adopts by reference the definition of earned income in section 911(d)(2).

Table 11. (Continued)

Description of provision	Wording of provision	Interaction with section 911
26 U.S.C § 1(g)(2)(A)(ii)(ll), (4)(A)(i).	This applies to certain children who did not have earned income that exceeded half of their support.	
Alternative minimum tax treatment of unearned income of minor children 26 U.S.C. § 59(j)(1)(A)	For children for whose income is taxed at their parent's rate, the allowable exemption under the alternative minimum tax cannot exceed the sum of the child's earned income and a set amount.	This provision adopts by reference the definition of earned income in section 911(d)(2).
Treatment of community income property 26 U.S.C § 66 (d)(1).	A married couple may earn community income as defined under the community property laws of a U.S. state or possession or a foreign country. If the spouses live apart at all times during the calendar year, do not file a joint return, have earned income which is community income, and do not transfer any portion of that earned income between themselves, then the community income is treated in accordance with section 879(a).	This provision adopts by reference the definition of earned income in section 911(d)(2).
Accident and health plans 26 U.S.C § 105(h)(3)(B)(v).	In general, employees can exclude certain health benefits offered by their employers from their income. However, certain highly compensated employees may not exclude the value of health benefits in certain cases. If health benefits are provided under a self-insured medical expense reimbursement plan which discriminates in favor of highly	This provision adopts by reference the definition of earned income in section 911(d)(2).

Description of provision	Wording of provision	Interaction with section 911
	compensated individuals, a portion of those benefits may not be excludable. When determining whether a plan is discriminatory, certain classes of employees need not be considered, including employees who have not completed three years of service, employees under the age of 25, part-time and seasonal employees, and nonresident alien employees who received no U.S.-source earned income from the employer.	
Qualified pension, profit-sharing, and stock bonus plans minimum coverage requirements 26 U.S.C. § 410(b)(3)(C)	Employers may establish qualified pension, profit-sharing or stock bonus plans (such as 401(k) plans) with certain tax advantages. A plan is not a qualified plan unless it meets certain requirements, including minimum coverage requirements. When determining whether a trust meets the minimum coverage requirements, certain classes of employees can be excluded, including nonresident alien employees who received no U.S.-source earned income from the employer.	This provision adopts by reference the definition of earned income in section 911(d)(2).
Qualified pension, profit-sharing, and stock bonus plans definitions and special rules 26 U.S.C. § 414(q)(8)	Employers may establish qualified pension, profit-sharing or stock bonus plans (such as 401(k) plans) with certain tax advantages. A plan is not a qualified plan unless it meets certain requirements, including minimum coverage	This provision adopts by reference the definition of earned income in section 911(d)(2).

Table 11. (Continued)

Description of provision	Wording of provision	Interaction with section 911
	requirements. If an employer is operating separate lines of business during a year, the employer may apply the minimum coverage requirements to each separate line of business. Nonresident alien employees who received no U.S.-source income from the employers are not considered employees for purposes of determining who highly compensated employees are and for determining whether the employer is engaged in a separate line of business.	
Exempt organizations 26 U.S.C § 505(b)(2)(E)	Organizations organized and operated for certain purposes are tax exempt. Tax exempt organizations include voluntary employee beneficiary associations providing certain benefits and trusts to provide group legal services. If these types of exempt organizations are part of a plan, they must meet certain additional requirements to maintain their tax exempt status, including that the plan of which they are a part be nondiscriminatory. When determining whether a plan is discriminatory, certain classes of employees need not be considered, including employees who have not completed three years of	This provision adopts by reference the definition of earned income in section 911(d)(2).

Description of provision	Wording of provision	Interaction with section 911
	service, employees under the age of 21, less than half-time and seasonal employees, and nonresident alien employees who received no U.S.-source earned income from the employer.	
Group-term life insurance provided by an employer 26 U.S.C § 79(d)(3)(B)(iv)	Employer provided group-term life insurance for employees is excludable from the income of the employees up to a certain amount. This exclusion is not available for certain key employees if the plan is discriminatory. When determining whether a plan is discriminatory, certain classes of employees need not be considered, including employees who have not completed three years of service, part-time and seasonal employees, and nonresident alien employees who received no U.S.-source earned income from the employer.	This provision adopts by reference the definition of earned income in section 911(d)(2).
Passive activity losses and credits 26 U.S.C § 469(e)(3)	In general, taxpayers may not take losses from passive activities in excess of aggregate income from passive activities or certain credits from passive activities in excess of regular tax liability allocable to all passive activities. When calculating income or loss from a passive activity, earned income is not taken into account.	This provision adopts by reference the definition of earned income in section 911(d)(2)(A), but not subsection 911(d)(2)(B).
Community income of nonresident alien individuals	A married couple may earn community income as defined under the community property	This provision adopts by reference the definition of earned

Table 11. (Continued)

Description of provision	Wording of provision	Interaction with section 911
26 U.S.C § 879(a)(1)	laws of a U.S. state or possession or a foreign country. If one or both spouses of a married couple are nonresident aliens, any community income that is earned income (other than trade or business income and a partner's distributive share of partnership income) is treated as income of the spouse who rendered the personal service.	income in section 911(d)(2).
Tax on group health plans which fail to satisfy continuation coverage requirements 26 U.S.C. § 4980B(g)(1)(C)	Group health plans which fail to meet certain continuation coverage requirements with respect to any qualified beneficiary are subject to a tax. A nonresident alien who received no U.S.-source earned income is not considered a qualified beneficiary when determining whether this requirement tax is imposed.	This provision adopts by reference the definition of earned income in section 911(d)(2).
Source rules for personal property sales 26 U.S.C § 865(g)(1)(A)(i)(l)	In general, income from the sale of personal property by a U.S. resident is sourced to the United States and the sale of personal property by a nonresident is sourced outside the United States. For purposes of this provision, an individual is a U.S. resident if he or she is a U.S. citizen or alien resident and who does not have a tax home in a foreign country or is a nonresident alien with a tax home in the United States.	This provision adopts by reference the definition of tax home in section 911(d)(3).

Description of provision	Wording of provision	Interaction with section 911
Residence and source rules involving possessions 26 U.S.C. § 937(a)(2)	In general, to be a bona fide resident of Guam, American Samoa, the Northern Mariana Islands, Puerto Rico, or the U.S. Virgin Islands, an individual must meet two requirements. First, the individual must be present for at least 183 days during the taxable year in that possession. Second, the individual must not have a tax home outside the possession where they were present for 183 days and not have a closer connection to the United States or a foreign country than to the possession.	This provision adopts by reference the section 911(d)(3), but without regard to the second sentence of section 911(d)(3).
Treatment of certain foreign currency transactions 26 U.S.C § 988(a)(3)(B)(i)(l)	In general, the source of ordinary income or loss from foreign currency transaction is determined, in part, by the residency of the taxpayer on whose books the relevant asset, liability, or item of income is properly reflected. For purposes of this provision, an individual's residency is the country in which the individual's tax home is located.	This provision adopts by reference the definition of tax home in section 911(d)(3).
Penalty under the requirement to maintain minimum essential coverage 26 U.S.C. § 5000A(f)(4)(A)	Individuals who do not maintain minimum essential healthcare insurance coverage are subject to a penalty. An individual is considered to have minimum essential coverage for any month in which the individual's tax home is in a foreign country and who is a bona fide resident	This provision adopts by reference section 911(d)(1) which provides that a qualified individual is an individual who is a bona fide resident of a foreign country or countries for the entire year or is

Table 11. (Continued)

Description of provision	Wording of provision	Interaction with section 911
	of a foreign country or countries for the entire year or is present in a foreign country or countries during at least 330 full days during that year.	present in a foreign country or countries during at least 330 full days during that year.
Resident alien and nonresident alien defined. 26 U.S.C § 7701(b)(3)(B)(ii)	In general, an alien individual is considered a resident alien of the United States if he or she meets certain requirements, including the substantial presence test. An individual will not be considered to meet the substantial presence test if he or she is present in the United States on fewer than 183 days during the current year, has a tax home in a foreign country (as defined in section 911(d)(3) without regard to the second sentence thereof), and has a closer connection to that foreign country than the United States.	This provision adopts by reference the definition of tax home in the first sentence of section 911(d)(3), but without regard to the second sentence of section 911(d)(3).

Source: GAO analysis of the United States Code.

Appendix III. Comparison of Tax Costs of U.S. and Non-U.S. Workers under the Foreign Earned Income Exclusion in Different Hypothetical Host Countries and at Different Income Levels

U.S. overseas workers' tax costs can vary across locations, and exceed the tax liabilities of non-U.S. workers. The foreign earned income exclusion (FEIE) can eliminate the U.S. income tax liability for some taxpayers residing overseas with foreign earned income. However, taxpayers with foreign earned income higher than the FEIE limit can, after applying the FEIE, incur a U.S. tax liability, in addition to the taxes they may owe to the foreign host nation. Tables 12 and 13 compare the tax liabilities of U.S. and non-U.S. workers in three hypothetical locations with varying effective tax rates. For each of the three locations, or host countries, both the U.S. and non-U.S. workers are assumed to be in a country other than their home country. The example in table 12 uses a level of foreign earned income sufficiently low that application of the FEIE eliminates the U.S. worker's U.S. tax liability. Table 13 uses a higher level of foreign earned income, illustrating that after applying the FEIE, the U.S. worker can incur a U.S. tax liability in addition to the taxes he or she may owe to the foreign host nation. In addition to comparing the tax liabilities of U.S. and non-U.S. workers in different locations, tables 12 and 13 also compare the U.S. worker's after-tax income abroad against what it would be were the worker employed in the United States. The tables also illustrate the U.S. worker's after tax income in three locations without use of the FEIE.

The examples included in the tables include certain assumptions, including that each employee (1) holds the same qualifications, (2) receives the same income, and (3) has a single tax filing status. The examples also assume the non-U.S. employee is not taxed by his or her home country on foreign-earned income, as the citizens of most other countries are not taxed by their country of citizenship if they reside in another country. The comparison focuses on home country tax rates for U.S. citizens and non-U.S. foreign nationals. U.S. citizens and non-U.S. foreign nationals would generally face the same local taxes as local citizens of the hypothetical host country. The U.S. effective tax rate listed is that which applies to the earned income level provided in the example, without application of the tax expenditure. Housing costs are not explicitly included in the example. Differences in housing costs can be offset by applicable housing exclusions or deductions. However, in some cases the differences in housing costs can affect overall tax liability. Finally, the example for table 13 assumes that the U.S. citizen working in country B would claim the foreign tax credit for any income not excluded through the FEIE, while, for both tables, the U.S citizen working in country C could claim the foreign tax credit instead of the tax expenditure since doing so would eliminate his or her U.S. tax obligation.

Table 12. Comparison of Tax Costs of U.S. and Non-U.S. Workers in Three Hypothetical Locations, at $107,600 Foreign Income Level

Country of employment	United States	Country A		Country B		Country C	
Effective tax rate	19%	0%		10%		25%	
Nationality of employee	U.S. Citizen	U.S. Citizen	Non-U.S. Foreign National	U.S. Citizen	Non-U.S. Foreign National	U.S. Citizen	Non-U.S. Foreign National
Earned income	$107,600	$107,600	$107,600	$107,600	$107,600	$107,600	$107,600
Less standard deduction $6,100 and one exemption $3,900	($10,000)	($10,000)	N/A	($10,000)	N/A	($10,000)	N/A
Less FEIE	N/A	($97,600)	N/A	($97,600)	N/A	N/A	N/A
Host country taxable income	N/A	$0	$0	$107,600	$107,600	$107,600	$107,600
Host country income tax	N/A	$0	$0	$10,760	$10,760	$26,900	$26,900
U.S. and total tax when FEIE is available							
U.S. taxable income	$97,600	$0	N/A	$0	N/A	$97,600	N/A
U.S. income tax after foreign tax credit	$20,628	$0	N/A	$0	N/A	$0	N/A
Total income after tax	$86,972	$107,600	$107,600	$96,840	$96,840	$80,700	$80,700
Difference between U.S. citizen after-tax income abroad and in the U.S.	N/A	$20,628	N/A	$9,868	N/A	($6,272)	N/A

Country of employment	**United States**	**Country A**		**Country B**		**Country C**	
Effective tax rate	**19%**	**0%**		**10%**		**25%**	
Nationality of employee	**U.S. Citizen**	**U.S. Citizen**	**Non-U.S. Foreign National**	**U.S. Citizen**	**Non-U.S. Foreign National**	**U.S. Citizen**	**Non-U.S. Foreign National**
Difference between U.S. citizen after-tax income and that of a non-U.S. citizen	N/A	$0	N/A	$0	N/A	$0	N/A
U.S. and total tax if FEIE if was not available							
U.S. taxable income	$97,600	$97,600	N/A	$97,600	N/A	$97,600	N/A
U.S. income tax after foreign tax credit	$20,628	$20,628	N/A	$9,868	N/A	$0	N/A
Total income after tax	$86,972	$86,972	$107,600	$86,972	$96,840	$80,700	$80,700
Difference between U.S. citizen after-tax income abroad and in the U.S.	N/A	$0	N/A	$0	N/A	($6,272)	N/A
Difference between U.S. citizen after-tax income and that of a non-U.S. citizen	N/A	($20,628)	N/A	($9,868)	N/A	$0	N/A

Source: GAO analysis.

Table 13. Comparison of Tax Costs of U.S. and Non-U.S. Workers in Three Hypothetical Locations, at $175,000 Foreign Income Level

Country of employment	United States	Country A		Country B		Country C	
Effective tax rate	**23%**	**0%**		**10%**		**25%**	
Nationality of employee	**U.S. Citizen**	**U.S. Citizen**	**Non-U.S. Foreign National**	**U.S. Citizen**	**Non-U.S. Foreign National**	**U.S. Citizen**	**Non-U.S. Foreign National**
Earned income	$175,000	$175,000	$175,000	$175,000	$175,000	$175,000	$175,000
Less standard deduction $6,100 and one exemption $3,900	($10,000)	($10,000)	N/A	($10,000)	N/A	($10,000)	N/A
Less FEIE	N/A	($97,600)	N/A	($97,600)	N/A	N/A	N/A
Host country taxable income	N/A	$0	$0	$175,000	$175,000	$175,000	$175,000
Host country income tax	N/A	$0	$0	$17,500	$17,500	$43,750	$43,750
U.S. and total tax when FEIE is available							
U.S. taxable income	$165,000	$67,400	N/A	$67,400	N/A	$165,000	N/A
Foreign Earned Income excluded	N/A	$97,600	N/A	$97,600	N/A	NA	N/A
U.S. income tax (no FEIE or foreign tax credit)	$39,493	$39,493	N/A	$39,493	N/A	$39,493	N/A
U.S. tax on excluded income	N/A	$20,628	N/A	$20,628	N/A	N/A	N/A
U.S. income tax after FEIE	$39,493	$18,865	N/A	$18,865	N/A	$39,493	N/A
Foreign tax allocable to excluded income	N/A	$0	N/A	$9,760	N/A	N/A	N/A
U.S. income tax after foreign tax credit	$39,493	$18,865	N/A	$9,105	N/A	$0	N/A

Country of employment	United States	Country A		Country B		Country C	
Effective tax rate	**23%**	**0%**		**10%**		**25%**	
Nationality of employee	**U.S. Citizen**	**U.S. Citizen**	**Non-U.S. Foreign National**	**U.S. Citizen**	**Non-U.S. Foreign National**	**U.S. Citizen**	**Non-U.S. Foreign National**
Total income after tax	$135,507	$156,135	$175,000	$148,395	$157,500	$131,250	$131,250
Difference between U.S. citizen after-tax income abroad and in the U.S.	N/A	$20,628	N/A	$12,888	N/A	($4,257)	N/A
Difference between U.S. citizen after-tax income and that of a non-U.S. citizen	N/A	($18,865)	N/A	($9,105)	N/A	$0	N/A
U.S. and total tax if FEIE if was not available							
U.S. taxable income	$165,000	$165,000	N/A	$165,000	N/A	$165,000	N/A
U.S. income tax after foreign tax credit	$39,493	$39,493	N/A	$21,993	N/A	$0	N/A
Total income after tax	$135,507	$135,507	$175,000	$135,507	$157,500	$131,250	$131,250
Difference between U.S. citizen after-tax income abroad and in the U.S.	N/A	$0	N/A	$0	N/A	($4,257)	N/A
Difference between U.S. citizen after-tax income and that of a non-U.S. citizen	N/A	($39,493)	N/A	($21,993)	N/A	$0	N/A

Source: GAO analysis.

Appendix IV. Assessment of the Current Tax Expenditure and Four Alternatives

Using criteria from our tax expenditure evaluation guide, we evaluated whether the tax expenditure[81]

- generates net economic benefits for society;
- is fair and equitable;
- is simple, transparent, and administrable; and
- is achieving its purpose.

The tax expenditure affects a variety of resource allocation decisions; it also affects equity in several different ways. Some of these effects are positive, while others are negative, and the magnitudes of all these effects are unknown. As a result, the tax expenditure's overall effect is uncertain.

Does the Tax Expenditure Generate Net Economic Benefits for Society?

A tax system reduces economic efficiency to the extent that it affects the relative prices of goods, services, or factors of production, and thereby induces individuals or businesses to alter economic decisions.[82] No tax system can avoid affecting some relative prices to some extent; however, it is important to minimize these price effects unless they are intended to achieve some other beneficial social purpose. We found that the tax expenditure had effects on the following.

Choices about where to work and who to hire: The tax expenditure potentially influences the choice of some U.S. citizens between working abroad or in the United States, because it lowers the total tax that these individuals would pay on foreign earned income. These tax reductions make working abroad in lower-tax countries more attractive to U.S. citizens than doing so otherwise would be and as a result, could interfere with the efficient allocation of U.S. labor between locations.[83]

The tax expenditure also potentially influences employers' choices as to whether they should fill positions abroad with U.S. citizens or with citizens of countries that do not tax earned income on a worldwide basis. The reduction in efficiency can occur when the employer hires a less productive worker for a lower pretax salary than the U.S. citizen would demand, due to the foreign worker paying no tax to his home country. The tax expenditure counteracts these effects, but we found no evidence in the economic literature that would indicate how the magnitude of the counteracting effects compares to the negative efficiency effects we discussed earlier. Consequently, we are not able to say whether the tax expenditure improves or reduces overall economic efficiency.

Differences in costs of living: Tax relief may be justified for U.S. citizens working in countries where the costs of living are significantly higher than the United States' highest-cost locations.[84] If these taxpayers' wages are sufficiently greater than they would earn at home (reflecting higher costs of living abroad), they may be pushed into higher tax brackets. This increase in the tax bracket is another way that the tax system could reduce efficiency by affecting location and hiring decisions. Tax relief targeted to the effects of this bracket change would remove an efficiency-reducing influence on U.S. citizens' employment decisions at a lower revenue cost than the more broad tax relief provided by the tax expenditure. This same efficiency problem arises domestically with respect to cost-of-living differences within the United States. Given that the U.S. tax system does not address this problem domestically, those who have proposed a means of addressing cost-of-living differences between the United States and foreign locations note that it may only be justified if the differences are much greater internationally than domestically.

Is the Tax Expenditure Fair and Equitable?

Equity is a subjective criterion. There are differing views on what an equitable tax system should look like, which can affect judgments on the fairness of a particular tax expenditure. Determining who benefits from the tax expenditure, and how those benefits affect equity, can be more complicated than simply identifying which taxpayers claim the tax expenditure. Three principles can inform judgments about the fairness of the tax expenditure:

Horizontal equity: Individuals with equal incomes and who are the same in terms of other characteristics deemed relevant to the ability to pay tax (such as number of dependents) should pay the same tax.

Vertical equity: Similar to horizontal equity, individuals with higher income or who have other characteristics that increase their ability to pay should pay more tax than those with less ability to pay. Identifying the characteristics that are relevant to an individual's ability to pay can involve value judgments. For that reason, among others, different observers may diverge in their assessments of how well a particular tax policy meets either of these equity criteria.[85]

Benefits received principle: An individual's tax payments should bear some relationship to the government benefits that individual receives. Once again, observers can differ in their judgments regarding the degree to which tax payments and benefits should be related, particularly because this criterion often conflicts with the other two equity criteria.

In order to apply any of these equity principles, it is necessary to identify individuals who benefit from the exclusion. This identification is complicated by the fact that the individual or business that is legally obligated to pay a tax—or that receives a tax benefit—is not always the one (or, at least, not the only one) that bears the ultimate burden of the tax or receives the ultimate benefit. The ultimate burden or benefit is known as the incidence of the tax policy, and it depends on how various individuals and businesses respond to the policy. For example, in the case of the tax expenditure, even though individual employees claim the exclusion on their own tax returns, the resulting reduction in their total taxes may make them willing to work abroad for a lower pretax income than they would have accepted without the tax expenditure. As a result, the foreign employers may share in at least some of the benefit by being able to pay lower salaries than would otherwise have been needed to hire U.S. citizens.

Determining the actual incidence of the tax expenditure would be difficult because it would require information on how two factors—the amount of labor that U.S. citizens are willing to supply to employers abroad and how those employers' demand for that particular type of labor—respond to changes in pretax and post-tax rates of compensation. We know of no study that has attempted to estimate such responsiveness. Given this uncertainty relating to the tax expenditure's incidence, it is difficult to draw conclusions about its effect on the equity of the tax system.

Conclusions about the tax expenditure's effect on horizontal equity depend, in part, on judgments about appropriate comparison groups. For U.S. policymakers, one relevant comparison is the treatment of U.S. citizens working abroad relative to similar U.S. citizens working in the United States. Unless all of the benefit from the tax expenditure is passed on to employers or unless those working abroad are deemed to be sufficiently different from their domestic counterparts due to either the potentially extreme cost-of-living differences discussed above or the differences in U.S. government services they receive, the tax expenditure violates the principle of horizontal equity between these two groups of individuals.

The tax expenditure decreases vertical equity to the extent that individuals who claim the exclusion tend to have higher incomes than those living in the United States, unless the incidence of the tax benefit falls entirely on employers. In comparison to an unlimited exclusion, the current design of the tax expenditure—specifically the dollar limit and the stacking rule[86]—moderates this negative effect.

In terms of the benefits principle, some of the experts we interviewed noted that U.S. citizens working abroad for the long term receive significantly smaller benefits from U.S. government services than those living in the United States, and that this difference may justify some tax relief for the former. Other experts noted that a large portion of federal revenues pay for services—such as national defense, foreign affairs, income maintenance, and basic research—that produce social or humanitarian benefits that are not directly apportioned to specific individuals. U.S. citizens living abroad likely benefit from some of these services. Many of those citizens also benefitted from years of public investment, for example, in their education, the cost of which is typically recaptured from citizens over their lifetimes. Moreover, some observers note that the choice to retain U.S. citizenship while living abroad provides some insurance with respect to being able to return and live within the United States whenever one wants. They maintain that citizens abroad should be willing to pay some tax for this insurance. Currently, U.S. citizens overseas must file a U.S. tax return and pay taxes owed unless they renounce their citizenship.[87] The National Taxpayer Advocate has reported that the numbers of those giving up their U.S. citizenship are growing.[88]

Citizens living abroad benefit from services provided by their host-countries' governments to which they pay taxes. Given that credits for foreign income taxes paid reduce the amount of tax that these citizens pay to the U.S federal government, any attempt to quantify discrepancies between federal benefits received and federal taxes paid should account for the foreign tax credit.[89]

The tax expenditure results in more comparable treatment between U.S. citizens working in a low-tax foreign country and foreign workers in that country that have similar characteristics; however, it is not clear that comparisons between these two groups would be of equal interest to U.S.

policymakers as the domestic taxpayer comparison. If this second comparison is considered relevant, the equity assessment would not be limited to a review of differences in the tax policies of various countries; it would also consider differences in the benefits that each government provides to citizens working abroad.

Is the Tax Expenditure Simple, Transparent, and Administrable?

There is widespread agreement that the U.S. worldwide tax system is complex and adds burden for taxpayers and IRS. The tax expenditure adds complexity with its eligibility rules and interactions with the foreign tax credit (FTC) and other tax provisions.

Transparency: Taxpayers may not fully understand their obligations under the tax expenditure. According to IRS, there is a common misconception that potentially excludable foreign earned income does not have to be reported on a U.S. tax return. IRS said that this misconception contributes to the tax gap, which is the difference between taxes owed and those paid on time.[90] However, data do not indicate the portion of the U.S. tax gap—most recently estimated by IRS at a net $385 billion as of 2006—that is attributable to international taxpayers who fail to file U.S. tax returns, underreport their foreign income, or fail to pay U.S. taxes owed. The National Taxpayer Advocate has called attention to the need to improve access and service for taxpayers located outside of the United States. IRS has undertaken research to study the needs of international taxpayers in helping them comply with their U.S. tax liabilities.[91]

Simplicity: According to some experts interviewed, the tax expenditure may simplify the tax compliance burdens of U.S. citizens abroad who would otherwise have to claim the FTC to avoid double taxation on foreign earned income. According to stakeholders and some experts we interviewed, the FTC can be more complex. However, this effect is uncertain for several reasons. First, we did not find evaluative studies that compare the compliance burden of the tax expenditure with the FTC. Second, taxpayers who claim the tax expenditure may bear the burden associated with claiming the FTC for capital income not covered by the tax expenditure. Additionally, taxpayers with only earned income may also do the FTC computations to determine which tax provision is the less costly option. Taxpayers with earned income exceeding the maximum exclusion face complexity in properly claiming both the tax expenditure and FTC.[92] Furthermore, taxpayers who claim the tax expenditure need to calculate their modified adjusted gross income (AGI) to determine eligibility for other tax benefits. In addition, taxpayers claiming the exclusion face additional recordkeeping to demonstrate that they meet the bona fide residence or to track days for the physical presence test.[93] Although the net effect of the tax expenditure on compliance burden may be uncertain, some experts have suggested that the compliance burden could be simplified by replacing the tax expenditure with a modified FTC or simplified FTC form.[94]

Administrability: IRS faces challenges in administering the tax expenditure, because IRS does not have the same level of information eporting on foreign source income as it does for U.S. source income to detect noncompliance. Like U.S. citizens working in the United States, citizens abroad working for U.S. companies would be subject to U.S. employer wage reporting and tax withholding.[95] However, IRS does not receive the same wage reports or tax withholding for U.S. citizens abroad working for foreign employers. Tax treaties and tax information exchange agreements with other nations can facilitate the exchange of taxpayer information. Additionally, recent information reporting requirements are an effort to improve transparency and provide tools for IRS to identify Americans abroad and address potential tax noncompliance.[96] However, the National Taxpayer Advocate reports and stakeholders we interviewed raised concerns that these reporting requirements add burden for citizens overseas as well as the third parties submitting the information.

IRS special compliance projects have found substantial noncompliance among high-risk taxpayers miscalculating or ineligible to claim benefits from the tax expenditure. Specifically, during 2009 through 2011, about 3,000 noncompliant tax returns identified by IRS special compliance projects were found to have miscalculated the exclusion or were not eligible resulting in an additional $21 million, according to the Treasury Inspector General for Tax Administration.[97] IRS said audits of exclusion claims are factually intensive and require information, for example, about a taxpayer's travel and domestic ties. The Treasury Inspector General for Tax Administration has reported on the challenges in administering the bona fide residence and physical presence tests.[98] IRS began including international taxpayers in its National Research Program in 2008 and plans to use the results to target enforcement on noncompliant taxpayers.[99]

How Well Does the Tax Expenditure Achieve Its Purposes?

As discussed earlier, the tax expenditure's effect on hiring and employment decisions is uncertain. There is little evidence to indicate that the tax expenditure could have more than a limited effect on exports. Moreover, there is no evidence to indicate that this effect is positive or that it would exceed any effect that the tax expenditure has on imports. Thus, it is not clear if the special tax relief for the relatively small population of U.S citizens living and working abroad positively benefits the overall well-being of the United States.

Some Alternatives to the Tax Expenditure Would Increase Efficiency and Equity, While the Effect of Others Would Depend on Details of the Reform

An assessment of the tax expenditure against criteria for good tax policy leaves room for debate regarding potential alternatives to improve the efficiency and equity as well as reduce complexity for taxpayers and IRS. Alternatives to the current tax expenditure range from eliminating it entirely—as proposed in several deficit reduction and tax reform proposals—to removing the maximum limit on the exclusion. We also considered alternatives to target tax relief to high cost areas and address the benefits received principle.[100]

Alternative: Eliminating the Tax Expenditure

The net effect on economic efficiency of eliminating the tax expenditure and taxing all foreign earned income is uncertain. This alternative would largely remove the influence of taxes on location decisions by U.S. citizens to work abroad, which would increase efficiency; however, at the same time, it would decrease efficiency by increasing the effect of the differential tax treatment by the United States and other countries on businesses' decisions regarding whom to hire for positions abroad. The effect of the alternative on equity is also uncertain. Elimination could be viewed as improving equity if two conditions are met: (1) there are few or no foreign locations where living costs are significantly higher than in the highest-cost locations within the United States, and (2) the additional federal taxes (in excess of the amounts offset by foreign tax credits) are broadly commensurate with the benefits that U.S. citizens working abroad receive from the U.S. government. If either of these conditions is not met, then some form of tax relief may be justified on equity grounds.

The effect on compliance burden will vary with the circumstances of the taxpayers. Eliminating the exclusion could increase the compliance burdens of some taxpayers who currently use the exclusion rather than the FTC to the extent that the FTC form is more complicated than the FEIE form. However, it would not significantly affect the compliance burden of taxpayers with earned income exceeding the exclusion limit or investment income who already use the FTC. IRS officials said that repealing the tax expenditure would simplify challenges associated with the FEIE bona fide residence and physical presence tests that do not apply to the FTC. Citizens working abroad in lower tax countries would face higher taxes. Those facing higher taxes or compliance costs may choose not to comply, and noncompliance could undercut the expected revenue gain from repeal.[101]

Alternative: Targeting Tax Relief for Extreme Cost of Living Differences

Economic efficiency and equity could be improved by modifying the current tax expenditure design or replacing it with an alternative tax relief that adjusts for foreign costs of living that significantly exceed those in the highest-cost U.S. locations. One approach would be to make Treasury responsible for annually determining the amount by which costs of living in foreign locations may exceed those in the highest-cost U.S. locations and for publishing adjustment factors for determining tax liabilities.[102] Whether a system of cost-of-living adjustments would be more burdensome for Treasury or taxpayers than the current tax expenditure, Alternative: Targeting Tax Relief Based on Benefits Received and Obligations as Citizens which already has some adjustment for higher housing expenses, depends on the degree of accuracy and completeness desired in the adjustments.[103] The federal revenue change would depend on the cost of tax reductions targeted to citizens working in higher cost foreign areas in place of the current preferential treatment for all citizens working abroad, and—depending on policy priorities and preferences—the redesign could aim for the same or a lower overall cost to the federal government.

Alternative: Targeting Tax Relief Based on Benefits Received and Obligations as Citizens

It would be difficult to design an alternative to the tax expenditure that better targeted tax relief based on benefits received. The tax expenditure itself is not designed specifically to address the benefits received principle, and the federal income tax in general is not based on the benefits received principle. Indeed, it would be very difficult to incorporate the principle in a tax that funds such a broad array of functions, many of which provide broad social benefits. Moreover, the values of these benefits are not easily allocable to specific individuals. Any attempt to determine a fair reduction in federal tax obligations of U.S. citizens living abroad relative to similar citizens living in the United States would involve a considerable amount of value judgment. Depending on policy priorities and preferences, any redesign targeted for reduced benefits received by citizens working overseas could aim for the same or a lower overall cost to the federal government. A revision deemed to result in a more equitable distribution of the tax burden would not necessarily have negative consequences for economic efficiency. The effects of the revision on simplicity and administrability would largely depend on the extent to which it is designed to account for the characteristics of individual taxpayers. One possible change in the current tax expenditure design would be to increase the time abroad required for eligibility. This would target tax relief to those abroad for longer periods. [104]

Alternative: Uncapping the Exclusion

Removing the maximum limit on the exclusion—that is, uncapping the tax expenditure—and excluding all foreign earned income from taxation would have multiple counteracting effects on employment decisions. These effects would be opposite to those that would result from eliminating the tax expenditure. In this case, inefficiency due to tax effects on location decisions would increase, while inefficiency due to the tax effects on hiring would decrease. Once again, because the relative magnitudes of the counteracting effects are indeterminable, the net effect on overall economic efficiency would be uncertain. The effect on equity will depend on value judgments. Uncapping the tax expenditure could be viewed as reducing both horizontal and vertical equity because it would reduce the federal tax liabilities of some high-income U.S. citizens working in countries with effective rates of income tax below that of the United States, regardless of the cost of living differences. On the other hand, it would increase equity if U.S. citizens working abroad are viewed as receiving no benefits for which they should pay federal taxes. To the extent that the exclusion is easier to use than the FTC, uncapping the exclusion could simplify compliance burdens for citizens abroad with only earned income, although they would still have to file a U.S. tax return to claim the tax benefit. However, uncapping the exclusion could compound the challenge that IRS has in administering the tax expenditure, given the misconception that those with excluded income do not have to file and report income to IRS. According to some experts we interviewed, uncapping the exclusion could create incentives for higher-income professionals to move abroad to deliver their services and to shift some investment income to be paid as earned income. It would also reduce federal tax revenue, and any perceived unfairness could erode voluntary compliance for domestic taxpayers. Experiences of other countries that do not tax foreign earned income may be useful in adopting tax rules and compliance practices to prevent or limit income shifting to lower tax countries.[105]

Uncapping the exclusion and not taxing any foreign earned income would be consistent with broader proposals to change the current U.S. worldwide system of taxation into a territorial or source-based income tax system. One proposal to move from "citizen-based" to "resident-based" taxation would exclude all foreign income for individuals living abroad; this could make the tax expenditure unnecessary.[106] Such an approach would impose a departure tax for citizens working abroad who reside in a foreign country for a minimum period of time.[107] Some proposals have implications not only for U.S. individual income tax filing but also for information reporting about foreign financial accounts and assets that are beyond the scope of this report. The larger debate about broader changes to the U.S. international tax system focuses chiefly on the taxation of corporate income, but such reforms may have implications for the tax treatment of the wage income of U.S. citizens working abroad that are beyond the scope of this report.[108]

End Notes

[1] GAO, *Government Performance and Accountability: Tax Expenditures Represent a Substantial Federal Commitment and Need to Be Reexamined*, GAO-05-690 (Washington, D.C.: Sept. 23, 2005), and *Tax Policy: Tax Expenditures Deserve More Scrutiny*, GAO/GGD/AIMD-94-122 (Washington, D.C.: June 3, 1994).

[2] See GAO, *Corporate Tax Expenditures: Evaluations of Tax Deferrals and Graduated Tax Rates*, GAO-13-789 (Washington, D.C.: Sept. 16, 2013); *Tax Expenditures: Background and Evaluation Criteria and Questions,* GAO-13-167SP (Washington, D.C.: Nov. 29, 2012); *Designing Evaluations: 2012 Revision*, GAO-12-208G (Washington, D.C.: January 2012); and *Executive Guide: Effectively Implementing the Government Performance and Results Act,* GAO/GGD-96-118 (Washington, D.C.: June 1996).

[3] GAO, *Understanding the Tax Reform Debate: Background, Criteria & Questions*, GAO-05-1009SP (Washington, D.C.: September 2005). This report describes how the criteria can be used to evaluate tax policy.

[4] Unless otherwise noted, all percentage estimates based on the SOI have 95 percent confidence intervals that are within 10 percentage points of the estimate itself, and all numerical

estimates other than percentages have 95 percent confidence intervals that are within 10 percent of the estimate itself.

[5] In our reporting of expert and stakeholder views, we refer to "most" experts or stakeholders as representing 7 or more; "about half" as representing 4 to 6; and "several" or "some" as representing 2 or 3.

[6] GAO-13-167SP. Our tax expenditure evaluation guide outlines a series of questions and criteria that can be used to evaluate tax expenditures. To develop the questions, we reviewed our prior work on tax expenditures, tax reform, results-oriented government, and program evaluation and interviewed experts in tax policy and program evaluation. GAO-05-1009SP summarizes the long-standing criteria used to evaluate tax policy.

[7] Permanent resident aliens are required to file U.S. tax returns on their worldwide income, generally using the same forms as U.S. citizens, regardless of where they reside. Nonresident aliens are required to file U.S. tax returns on their U.S. source income in some circumstances, using Forms 1040NR. (Forms 1040NR are counted and tracked separately.)

[8] 26 U.S.C. § 901. Taken as a credit on Form 1116, *Foreign Tax Credit*, foreign income taxes reduce the U.S. tax liability dollar for dollar. Taken as a deduction on Form 1040, *Schedule A, Itemized Deductions*, foreign income taxes reduce the U.S. taxable income.

[9] This report focuses on U.S. federal income taxation. Some states also tax foreign earned income. According to tax advisor materials, among the states that tax citizens overseas are California, New Mexico, South Carolina, and Virginia.

[10] 26 U.S.C. 911(b)(1)(B)(ii).

[11] 26 U.S.C. § 911(d)(2).

[12] For purposes of the FEIE, "tax home" has the same meaning which it has for purposes of IRC section 162(a)(2) (relating to travel expenses away from home). Thus, an individual's tax home is considered to be located at his regular or principal (if more than one regular) place of business or, if the individual has no regular or principal place of business because of the nature of the business, then at his regular place of abode in a real and substantial sense. An individual shall not, however, be considered to have a tax home in a foreign country for any period for which the individual's abode is in the United States. Temporary presence of the individual in the United States does not necessarily mean that the individual's abode is in the United States during that time. Maintenance of a dwelling in the United States by an individual, whether or not that dwelling is used by the individual's spouse and dependents, does not necessarily mean that the individual's abode is in the United States. 26 C.F.R. § 1.911-2(b).

[13] The term "foreign country" includes any territory under the sovereignty of a government other than that of the United States. 26 C.F.R. § 1.911-2(h). For this purpose, it does not include Antarctica or U.S. possessions such as Puerto Rico, Guam, the Commonwealth of the Northern Mariana Islands, the U.S. Virgin Islands, American Samoa, and Johnston Island. It also does not include international waters or the airspace above them.

[14] For purposes of section 911, residence is determined by applying, to the extent feasible, the principles of section 871 of the tax code and regulations thereunder, which involve factors including the taxpayer's intention, establishment of a home in the foreign country for an indefinite time, and participation in the activities of the community. Bona fide residence in a foreign country or countries for an uninterrupted period may be established, even if temporary visits are made during the period to the United States or elsewhere on vacation or business. 26 C.F.R. § 1.911-2(c). An individual would not be considered a resident if a statement was submitted to the tax authorities of the foreign country indicating nonresidency and the foreign country did not subject the individual to foreign income taxation.

[15] If an individual's tax home was in a foreign country and he or she was a bona fide resident of, or physically present in, a foreign country and had to leave because of war, civil unrest, or similar adverse conditions, the minimum time requirements specified under the bona fide residence and physical presence tests may be waived. If an individual has not met either the

physical presence test or the bona fide residence test by the due date of his or her return, the individual can file his or her return timely without claiming the exclusion and then file an amended return after qualifying.

[16] The sum of the FEIE and the housing exclusion or deduction is limited to total foreign earned income.

[17] 26 U.S.C. § 911(c)(1)(B). Eligible housing expenses include rent, the fair rental value of housing provided in kind by the employer, utilities (other than telephone charges), real and personal property insurance, rental of furniture and accessories, repairs, and residential parking. Expenses must be reasonable and incurred during the period eligible for the exclusion. 26 C.F.R. § 1.911-4(a), (b).

[18] Treasury updates the local maximums each year using publicly available information from the Living Quarters Allowances Tables prepared by the Department of States' Office of Allowances. See U.S. Department of State, *Summary of Allowances and Benefits for S.G. Civilians Under The Department of State Standardized Regulations (DSSR)*, accessed January 24, 2014, http://aoprals.state.gov/content.asp?content_id=134&menu_id=75. IRS publishes these amounts in bulletins. See Internal Revenue Service, *Determination of Housing Cost Amount Eligible for Exclusion or Deduction for 2013,* Internal Revenue Bulletin 2013-21 (Washington D.C.: May 20, 2013).

[19] 26 U.S.C. § 911(f).

[20] For example, if a taxpayer excludes $80,000 of foreign earned income and has $20,000 in other taxable income, he will pay tax on the $20,000 at the tax rate applicable to a person with $100,000 in income rather than at the rate applicable to a person with $20,000 in income.

[21] On a joint return, one or both spouses may have claimed the FEIE. When two spouses live apart and maintain separate households and both qualify to claim the FEIE, the foreign housing exclusion, or the foreign housing deduction, they must file two separate Forms 2555.

[22] Internal Revenue Service, *Individual Income Tax Returns 2011*, Publication 1304 (Washington D.C.: August 2013).

[23] Foreign Earned Income Act of 1978, Pub. L. 95–615, § 208. 92 Stat. 3097, 3108, as amended by the Economic Recovery Tax Act of 1981, Pub. L. 97–34, §114, 95 Stat. 172, 195–196; and the Revenue Reconciliation Act of 1990, Pub. L. 101–508, §11833, 104 Stat. 1388, 1388–560. *See* 26 U.S.C. § 911 note.

[24] Scott Hollenbeck and Maureen Keenan Kahr, *Individual Foreign-Earned Income and Foreign Tax Credit, 2006*, Statistics of Income (SOI) Bulletin (Washington D.C.: Internal Revenue Service, Spring 2009).

[25] While, in general, the tax expenditure lists Treasury and JCT publish annually are similar, they differ somewhat in the number of tax expenditures reported, and the estimated revenue losses for particular expenditures. The organizations use different (1) income tax baselines, (2) *de minimis* amounts (which is the minimum revenue loss threshold for Treasury and JCT to report a tax expenditure), and (3) economic and technical assumptions. For more information on how Treasury and JCT estimate revenue loss, see appendix III in GAO-05-690.

[26] Changes in taxpayer behavior are taken into account when Treasury and JCT prepare revenue estimates for proposed legislation.

[27] Changes in economic conditions and estimation techniques can affect revenue loss estimates for tax expenditures, making them differ from year to year. Also, legislation affecting tax rates or the tax structure affects tax expenditure estimates. When statutory rates increase, a taxpayer's ability to avoid tax on a portion of income is worth more; consequently, tax expenditures are worth more. Likewise, when rates decrease, tax expenditures are worth relatively less.

[28] Office of Management and Budget, *Analytical Perspectives, Budget of the United States Government, Fiscal Year 2015* (Washington, D.C.: 2014); and Joint Committee on

Taxation, *Estimates of Federal Tax Expenditures for Fiscal Years 2012-2017*, JCS-1-13 (Washington, D.C.: Feb. 1, 2013).

[29] See U.S. Congress, Senate Committee on the Budget, *Tax Expenditures: Compendium of Background Material on Individual Provisions*, S. Prt. 111-58 (Washington, D.C.: Congressional Research Service, December 2012). For more on the tax expenditure's history, see Michael S. Kirsch, "Taxing Citizens in a Global Economy," *New York University Law Review*, vol. 82, no. 2 (2007).

[30] See Brookfield Global Relocation Services, *Global Relocation Trends: 2013 Survey Report* (Chicago, IL: Brookfield Consulting Services Group, 2013), and Cartus, *2012 Trends in Global Relocation,* Global Mobility Policy and Practices Survey (Cartus Corporation: May 2012).

[31] Besides cross-border exports, U.S. companies can also sell to foreign countries through affiliate sales abroad.

[32] Exec. Order No. 13534, 75 Fed. Reg. 12,433 (Mar. 11, 2010).

[33] Pub. L. No. 111-352, 124 Stat. 3866 (2011) (updating the Government Performance and Results Act of 1993, Pub. L. No. 103-62, 107 Stat. 285 (1993)). This act calls upon the Office of Management and Budget to develop long-term, outcome-oriented goals for a limited number of cross-cutting policy areas, and to provide information on how they will be achieved. Under the act, tax expenditures are to be included in identifying the range of federal agencies and activities that contribute to crosscutting goals. 31 U.S.C. § 1115(a)(2).

[34] For more on our work on export promotion, see our export promotion Key Issue page, at http://www.gao.gov/key_issues/export_promotion/issue_summary. The Key Issue page highlights our relevant reports and multimedia content.

[35] A new crosscutting goal focuses on increasing foreign direct investment in the United States.

[36] The U.S. Census Bureau has typically counted overseas military and federal civilian employees and their dependents, but it has usually excluded private citizens residing abroad. As of January 2013, the U.S. Department of State estimated 6.8 million American citizens live abroad.

[37] The balance filed as head of household, married filing separately, or surviving spouse. The percentage estimates have 95 percent confidence intervals that are within 2 percentage points of the estimate itself.

[38] Out of FEIE filers, percent estimates for filers claiming a housing exclusion or housing deduction have 95 percent confidence intervals that are within 16 percent (within 3 percentage points) of the estimate itself.

[39] Most of the amount claimed was for the FEIE. For 2011, the maximum exclusion for foreign earned income was $92,900.

[40] The 2011 results in tables 3 and 4 are similar to prior analysis of tax year 2006 Statistics of Income data. See Eric Toder, "Taxes on Foreign Earned Income," *Tax Notes Today* (Washington, D.C.: Tax Policy Center, July 16, 2013), accessed February 10, 2014. http://www.urban.org/publications/1001689.html.

[41] Taxpayers who choose to claim the FEIE cannot double dip and claim the FTC for foreign taxes on the income excluded.

[42] Taxpayers that cannot use the full amount of qualified foreign taxes paid or accrued in the tax year are allowed a 1-year carryback and then a 10-year carryover of the unused foreign taxes.

[43] As of 2010, 16 countries had special tax incentives, such as deductions, exemptions, and reduced tax rates, for high-skilled workers. See Organisation for Economic Co-operation and Development, *Taxation and Employment*, OECD Tax Policy Studies, No. 21 (OECD Publishing, 2011) accessed July 25, 2013, http://dx.doi.org/10.1787/9789264120808-en.

[44] 26 U.S.C § 32(c)(1)(C).

[45] 26 U.S.C. § 911(d)(6).

[46] For example, see PricewaterhouseCoopers (PwC), *Economic Analysis of the Foreign Earned Income Exclusion* (National Economic Consulting: November 7, 2005); and John H. Mutti,

"The American Presence Abroad and U.S. Exports," *Southern Economic Journal*, vol. 47 (July 1980), pp. 40-50. These studies, however, have several weaknesses, which are discussed later in this report.

[47] Appendix III provides additional examples comparing the tax costs of U.S. and non-U.S. workers, at different income levels and different host country effective tax rates, and also compares the difference between U.S. worker's income tax liability in the United States and abroad.

[48] See Brookfield Global Relocation Services, *Global Relocation Trends: 2013 Survey Report* (Chicago, IL: Brookfield Consulting Services Group, 2013); KPMG International Cooperative, *Global Assignment Policies and Practices Survey* (International Executive Services: July 2013); and Cartus, *2012 Trends in Global Relocation,* Global Mobility Policy and Practices Survey (Cartus Corporation: May 2012).

[49] Commerce has studied the relationship between short-term business travel and exports, and found U.S. outbound international business travel has a positive effect on U.S. merchandise exports. See Maksim Belenkiy and David Riker, *U.S. International Business Travel: Its Impact on U.S. Merchandise Exports,* Manufacturing and Services Economics Brief (Washington, D.C.: Office of Competition and Economic Analysis, November 2012).

[50] See Performance.gov, "Cross-Agency Priority Goal: Exports" accessed May 30, 2013 http://goals.performance.gov/content/exports.

[51] Our prior reports drew on surveys of U.S. companies with foreign operations. Those results were not representative of all employers at that time and given changes in the global economy, are outdated. See GAO, *American Employment Abroad Discouraged By U.S. Income Tax Laws*, ID-81-27 (Washington, D.C.: Feb. 27, 1981), and *Tax Policy and Administration: Impact on Trade of Changes in Taxation of U.S. Citizens Employed Overseas*, ID-78-13 (Washington, D.C.: Feb. 21, 1978).

[52] Mutti, "American Presence Abroad."

[53] PricewaterhouseCoopers (PwC), *Economic Analysis*.

[54] John Tschetter, "Exports Support American Jobs: Updated Measure Will Quantify Progress As Global Economy Recovers," International Trade Research Report no. 1 (Washington, D.C.: Department of Commerce, International Trade Administration, Undated).

[55] See GAO, *Export-Import Bank: More Detailed Information about Its Jobs Calculation Methodology Could Improve Transparency*, GAO-13-446 (Washington, D.C.: May 23, 2013).

[56] Unless otherwise specified, the term "tax expenditure" here refers to the foreign earned income exclusion as well as the exclusion and deduction for excess foreign housing costs.

[57] Resources are used most efficiently when they provide the greatest possible benefit or well-being. The concept of economic efficiency recognizes that when resources are not underemployed, decisions about their use involve tradeoffs. See GAO-13-167SP and GAO-05-1009SP for a more detailed discussion of economic efficiency.

[58] If policymakers are concerned that tax rate differences across countries already cause inefficiencies that need to be addressed by U.S. tax policy, then the United States would also have to compensate U.S. citizens working in high-tax countries (to the extent that the taxes they pay there exceed what they would have paid in the United States).

[59] See U.S. Congress, Senate Committee on the Budget, *Tax Expenditures: Compendium of Background Material on Individual Provisions*, S. Prt. 112-45 (Washington, D.C.: Congressional Research Service, December 2012) and Jane G. Gravelle and Donald W. Kiefer, *U.S. Taxation of Citizens Working in Other Countries: An Economic Analysis* (Washington, D.C.: Congressional Research Service, Apr. 20, 1978).

[60] The ultimate burden or benefit is known as the incidence of the tax policy and it depends on how various individuals and businesses respond to the policy. In the case of the tax expenditure, even though individual employees claim the exclusion on their own tax returns, the resulting reduction in their total taxes may make them willing to work abroad for a lower pretax income than they would have accepted without the tax expenditure. As a

result, the employers may share in at least some of the benefit by being able to pay lower salaries than would otherwise have been needed to hire U.S. citizens.

[61] Determining the actual incidence of the FEIE would be difficult because it would require information on how two factors—the amount of labor that U.S. citizens are willing to supply to employers abroad and how those employers' demand for that particular type of labor— respond to changes in pretax and post-tax rates of compensation. We know of no study that has attempted to estimate such responsiveness.

[62] For taxpayers that have taxable income after claiming the FEIE and foreign housing exclusion, the applicable tax rate is determined by calculating taxable income without taking these exclusions into account. This stacking rule results in these taxpayers claiming the tax expenditure being subject to the same marginal tax rates as taxpayers with the same level of income who are not eligible for (or do not elect to claim) the tax expenditure.

[63] Expatriation tax provisions apply to U.S. citizens who have relinquished their citizenship and long-term residents who ceased to be lawful permanent residents. The rules that apply are based on the date of expatriation, as described in IRS Publication 519—*U.S. Tax Guide for Aliens* (available at http://www.irs.gov/publications/p519/ar01.html).

[64] Appendix IV contains additional detail on our assessment of transparency and simplicity for taxpayers and administrability for IRS.

[65] Tiffanie N. Reker, David C. Cico, and Saima S. Mehmood, *2012 Taxpayer Experience of Individuals Living Abroad: Service Awareness, Use, Preferences, and Filing Behaviors*, Research Study Report (Internal Revenue Service, W&I Research & Analysis: June 21, 2012).

[66] Treasury Inspector General for Tax Administration, *Improvements Are Needed to Reduce Erroneous Foreign Earned Income Exclusion Claims,* Reference Number 2010-40-091 (Washington, D.C.: Aug. 16, 2010).

[67] To identify and analyze alternative policy options, we conducted an extensive literature search and interviewed a range of stakeholders and experts; see appendix I for more on our methodology and a list of the options discussed with those we interviewed.

[68] The staff of the Joint Committee on Taxation estimate that repealing the exclusion would increase federal revenue by $6.2 billion in 2015 and $89 billion over 2014 through 2023; see Congressional Budget Office, *Options for Reducing the Deficit: 2014 to 2023 (Washington, D.C.: November 2013)*. Unlike a tax expenditure estimate, revenue estimates generally reflect changes in behavior by individuals and firms.

[69] Such an approach is discussed in Gravelle and Kiefer (1978). Certain cost differences— such as those relating to education and certain types of taxes—present complications that may not be adequately addressed by comparing available cost-of-living indexes.

[70] The Foreign Earned Income Act of 1978 replaced an income exclusion with a system of allowances for costs of living abroad, such as cost of living in general, housing, education, and home leave transportation. This system was replaced in 1981 with the income exclusion and separate housing exclusion.

[71] Currently, the physical presence test is for at least 330 days over a 12-month period. In the 1950s, the FEIE physical presence test was for 510 days (17 months) out of 18 consecutive months. In 1962, the exclusion was tiered allowing a larger exclusion for those overseas for 3 years or more.

[72] GAO, *International Taxation: Study Countries That Exempt Foreign-Source Income Face Compliance Risks and Burdens Similar to Those in the United States,* GAO-09-934 (Washington, D.C.: Sept. 15, 2009).

[73] American Citizens Abroad (ACA), *ACA Submission to the Senate Finance Committee on International Tax Reform* (Washington, D.C.: Jan. 15, 2014). ACA also supports increasing the current exclusion limit.

[74] Under the ACA proposal, an individual would be deemed to have disposed of property at its fair market value on the day of departure and then reacquired the property for the same amount immediately thereafter. The person would include in U.S. income the capital gain or

loss that resulted from the deemed disposition. Alternatively, the person could defer the tax without interest until his or her return to the United States.

[75] Subtitle A of Title V of the Hiring Incentives to Restore Employment Act (HIRE Act), commonly known as the Foreign Account Tax Compliance Act, requires foreign financial institutions to report on certain foreign financial accounts and offshore assets, while the Bank Secrecy Act and implementing regulations require individuals to report on certain foreign financial accounts and imposes penalties on the failure to meet these reporting requirements. 26 U.S.C. §§ 1471–1474; 31 U.S.C. § 5314; 31 C.F.R. §§ 1010.350, 1010.820.

[76] Forms 1040-NR are counted and tracked separately by IRS and are not part of the SOI sample. IRS officials told us that a small number of taxpayers claiming the FEIE incorrectly file a 1040NR.

[77] U.S. Congress, Senate Committee on the Budget, *Tax Expenditures: Compendium of Background Material on Individual Provisions*, S. Prt. 111-58 (Washington, D.C.: Congressional Research Service, December 2012).

[78] For an example of GAO work on the worldwide taxation of corporate income, see GAO, *Corporate Tax Expenditures: Evaluations of Tax Deferrals and Graduated Tax Rates*, GAO-13-789 (Washington, D.C.: Sept. 16, 2013).

[79] See GAO, *American Employment Abroad Discouraged By U.S. Income Tax Laws*, ID-81-27 (Washington, D.C.: Feb. 27, 1981), *Impact on Trade of Changes in Taxation of U.S. Citizens Employed Overseas*, ID-78-13 (Washington, D.C.: Feb. 21, 1978), and Jane G. Gravelle and Donald W. Kiefer, *U.S. Taxation of Citizens Working in Other Countries: An Economic Analysis*, CRS-78-91 (Washington: D.C.: Congressional Research Service, April 20, 1978).

[80] GAO, *Tax Expenditures: Background and Evaluation Criteria and Questions*, GAO-13-167SP (Washington D.C.: Nov. 29, 2012). Our tax expenditure evaluation guide outlines a series of questions and criteria that can be used to evaluate tax expenditures. To develop the questions, we reviewed our prior work on tax expenditures, tax reform, results-oriented government, and program evaluation and interviewed experts in tax policy and program evaluation. GAO, *Understanding the Tax Reform Debate: Background, Criteria, and Questions,* GAO-05-1009SP (Washington D.C.: September 2005) summarizes the long-standing criteria used to evaluate tax policy.

[81] Unless otherwise specified, the term "tax expenditure" here refers to the foreign earned income exclusion as well as the exclusion and deduction for excess foreign housing costs.

[82] Resources are used most efficiently when they provide the greatest possible benefit or well-being. The concept of economic efficiency recognizes that when resources are not underemployed, decisions about their use involve tradeoffs. See GAO, *Tax Expenditures: Background and Evaluation Criteria and Questions,* GAO-13-167SP (Washington, D.C.: Nov. 29, 2012) and *Understanding the Tax Reform Debate: Background, Criteria & Questions*, GAO-05-1009SP (Washington, D.C.: September 2005) for a more detailed discussion of economic efficiency.

[83] If policymakers are concerned that tax rate differences across countries already cause inefficiencies that need to be addressed by U.S. tax policy, then the United States would also have to compensate U.S. citizens working in high-tax countries (to the extent that the taxes they pay there exceed what they would have paid in the United States).

[84] See U.S. Congress, Senate Committee on the Budget, *Tax Expenditures: Compendium of Background Material on Individual Provisions*, S. Prt. 112-45 (Washington, D.C.: Congressional Research Service, December 2012) and Jane G. Gravelle and Donald W. Kiefer, *U.S. Taxation of Citizens Working in Other Countries: An Economic Analysis* (Washington, D.C.: Congressional Research Service, Apr. 20, 1978).

[85] Another value judgment relates to the progressivity of a tax—the degree to which taxes should increase as the ability to pay increases.

[86] For taxpayers that have taxable income after claiming the FEIE and foreign housing exclusion, the applicable tax rate is determined by calculating taxable income without taking these exclusions into account. This stacking rule results in these taxpayers claiming the tax expenditure being subject to the same marginal tax rates as taxpayers with the same level of income who are not eligible for (or do not elect to claim) the tax expenditure.

[87] Expatriation tax provisions apply to U.S. citizens who have relinquished their citizenship and long-term residents who ceased to be lawful permanent residents. The rules that apply are based on the date of expatriation, as described in IRS Publication 519—*U.S. Tax Guide for Aliens (available at http://www.irs.gov/publications/p519/ar01.html).*

[88] Taxpayer Advocate Service, *2012 Annual Report to Congress,* (Washington D.C.: Dec. 31, 2012). Based on analysis of IRS quarterly reports listing those giving up citizenship, the Taxpayer Advocate reported that expatriations increased substantially from 2008 to 2011. The latest IRS report available listed 1,001 citizens and long-term residents losing U.S. citizenship in the quarter ending March 31, 2014. 79 Fed. Reg. 25,176 (May 2, 2014).

[89] In the absence of the tax expenditure, some employers might raise the pretax salaries of its employees who are U.S. citizens to offset losses in services that the latter would incur by accepting a position abroad. As we noted in the discussion of incidence, the likelihood of this occurring is unknown. In such cases the tax expenditure does not provide any improvement in equity; it would simply reduce costs for those particular employers.

[90] For more on GAO's work on the tax gap, see our Tax Gap Key Issue page, at http://gao.gov/key_issues/tax_gap/issue_summary#t=1.

[91] Tiffanie N. Reker, David C. Cico, and Saima S. Mehmood, *2012 Taxpayer Experience of Individuals Living Abroad: Service Awareness, Use, Preferences, and Filing Behaviors*, Research Study Report (Internal Revenue Service, W&I Research & Analysis: June 21, 2012).

[92] Foreign earned income excluded cannot be deducted, excluded a second time, or used to claim a credit, so taxpayers are required to compute the fraction of foreign taxes that are not allocable to the excluded income.

[93] Treasury Inspector General for Tax Administration, *Improvements Are Needed to Reduce Erroneous Foreign Earned Income Exclusion Claims,* Reference Number 2010-40-091 (Washington, D.C.: Aug. 16, 2010).

[94] Whereas the form 2555 for the exclusion has an EZ version, the foreign tax credit form 1116 does not have an EZ version.

[95] Wages are subject to withholding to the extent that they exceed the amount of the exclusion. An exemption from withholding on excluded wages is available for citizens abroad but not resident aliens. Employers do not have to withhold U.S. taxes if they are required to withhold taxes for a foreign government.

[96] Subtitle A of Title V of the Hiring Incentives to Restore Employment Act (HIRE Act), commonly known as the Foreign Account Tax Compliance Act, requires foreign financial institutions to report on certain foreign financial accounts and offshore assets, while the Bank Secrecy Act and implementing regulations require individuals to report on certain foreign financial accounts and imposes penalties on the failure to meet these reporting requirements. 26 U.S.C. §§ 1471–1474; 31 U.S.C. § 5314; 31 C.F.R. §§ 1010.350, 1010.820.

[97] Treasury Inspector General for Tax Administration, *The Referral Process for Examinations of Tax Returns Claiming the Foreign Income Exclusion Needs to Be Improved,* Reference Number 2013-30-112 (Washington, D.C.: Sept. 27, 2013).

[98] Treasury Inspector General for Tax Administration, *Improvements Needed to Reduce Erroneous Claims.*

[99] The National Research Program uses audits of a stratified, random sample of tax returns to produce statistically valid estimates of noncompliance for the entire population of tax return filers. For tax years 2006 through 2010, IRS sampled each year about 450 international taxpayers in its National Research Program. IRS plans to use these results for workload

planning. The relatively small sample is not representative for estimating the international component of the tax gap.

[100] To identify and analyze alternative policy options, we conducted an extensive literature search and interviewed a range of stakeholders and experts; see appendix I for more on our methodology and a list of the options discussed with those we interviewed.

[101] The staff of the Joint Committee on Taxation estimate that repealing the exclusion would increase federal revenue by $6.2 billion in 2015 and $89 billion over 2014 through 2023; see Congressional Budget Office, *Options for Reducing the Deficit: 2014 to 2023* (Washington, D.C.: November 2013). Unlike a tax expenditure estimate, revenue estimates generally reflect changes in behavior by individuals and firms.

[102] Such an approach is discussed in Gravelle and Kiefer (1978). Certain cost differences— such as those relating to education and certain types of taxes—present complications that may not be adequately addressed by comparing available cost-of-living indexes.

[103] The Foreign Earned Income Act of 1978 replaced an income exclusion with a system of allowances for costs of living abroad, such as cost of living in general, housing, education, and home leave transportation. This system was replaced in 1981 with the income exclusion and separate housing exclusion.

[104] Currently, the physical presence test is for at least 330 days over a 12-month period. In the 1950s, the FEIE physical presence test was for 510 days (17 months) out of 18 consecutive months. In 1962, the exclusion was tiered, allowing a larger exclusion for those overseas for 3 years or more.

[105] GAO, *International Taxation: Study Countries That Exempt Foreign-Source Income Face Compliance Risks and Burdens Similar to Those in the United States,* GAO-09-934 (Washington, D.C.: Sept. 15, 2009).

[106] American Citizens Abroad, *ACA Submission to the Senate Finance Committee on International Tax Reform*, (Washington, D.C.: Jan. 15, 2014). ACA also supports increasing the current exclusion limit.

[107] Under the ACA proposal, an individual would be deemed to have disposed of property at its fair market value on the day of departure and then reacquired the property for the same amount immediately thereafter. The person would include in U.S. income the capital gain or loss that resulted from the deemed disposition. Alternatively, the person could defer the tax without interest until return to the United States. For other exit tax proposals, see Patrick W. Martin and Reuven Avi-Yonah, "Tax Simplification: The Need for Consistent Tax Treatment of All Individuals (Citizens, Lawful Permanent Residents and Non-Citizens Regardless of Immigration Status) Residing Overseas, Including the Repeal of U.S. Citizenship Based Taxation," *Procopio News Room* 09.17.2013 (San Diego, CA: Procopio, September 2013), accessed March 10, 2014, http://www.procopio.com/news/tax-simplification-the-need-for-consistent-tax-treatment-of-all-individuals-citizens-lawful-permanent-residents-and-non-citizens-regardless-of-immigration-status-residing-overseas-including-the-repeal-of-u.s.-citizenship-based-taxation; Bernard Schenider, "The End of Taxation without End: A New Tax Regime for U.S. Expatriates," *Virginia Tax Review, Vol. 32 No. 1* (London, UK: Queen Mary University of London, Summer 2012); and Cynthia Blum and Paula N. Singer, "A Coherent Policy Proposal for U.S. Residence-Based Taxation of Individuals," *Vanderbilt Journal of Transnational Law* vol. 41, no. 3 (2008).

[108] See Joint Committee on Taxation, *Present Law and Issues in U.S. Taxation of Cross-Border Income*, JCX-42-11 (Washington, D.C.: Sept. 6, 2011).

In: The Foreign Earned Income Tax Exclusion ISBN: 978-1-63321-974-8
Editor: Molly Milburn

Chapter 2

Individual Foreign-Earned Income and Foreign Tax Credit, 2011[*,†]

Scott Hollenbeck and Maureen Keenan Kahr

For 2011, the total amount of foreign-earned income reported by U.S. taxpayers grew in real terms by 32.3 percent, to over $54.2 billion. Foreign-source gross income reported by U.S. taxpayers reached nearly $170.0 billion for the year; total foreign tax credit claimed was just under $16.5 billion. Unless otherwise stated, the statistics reported in this article are based on data compiled from Form 2555, *Foreign Earned Income*, Form 2555-EZ, *Foreign Earned Income Exclusion*, Form 1116, *Foreign Tax Credit,* and Form 1040, *U.S. Individual Income Tax Return*. U.S. taxpayers file these forms with their individual income tax returns to report foreign-earned income and claim the foreign tax credit.

Foreign-Earned Income Highlights

In 2011, nearly 450,000 U.S. taxpayers living abroad reported just over $54.2 billion in foreign-earned income, an increase of 32.3 percent in real

[*] This is an edited, reformatted and augmented version of an article included in the Statistics of Income Bulletin - Spring 2014, issued by the U.S. Internal Revenue Service, June 2014.

[†] This article was written by Scott Hollenbeck and Maureen Keenan Kahr, economists with the Individual Research Section, under the direction of Mike Strudler, Chief.

terms from 2006 (the last time this study was done). U.S. taxpayers claimed more than $28.3 billion as a foreign-earned income exclusion on their tax returns for the year. Between 2006 and 2011, the inflation-adjusted amount of the foreign-earned income exclusion increased 38.4 percent, while the housing exclusion increased 5.8 percent, rising from just under $1.5 billion to nearly $1.6 billion for 2011 (Figure A).

Asian-based U.S. taxpayers reported the largest amount of total foreign-earned income ($24.9 billion) from any continent for 2011, a 52.2-percent increase in real growth from the $16.4 billion reported for 2006. This continued a decade of large increases reported on returns from Asia. For 2011, these returns represent approximately 46 percent of all the foreign-earned income reported by U.S. taxpayers, up from roughly 40 percent for 2006 and 36 percent for 2001. Some of this growth is attributable to returns with a tax home of Afghanistan with $3.0 billion reported in total foreign-earned income for 2011, after reporting $0.5 billion in 2006. Taxpayers based in Singapore also drove this growth, reporting a real increase of 129.4 percent (to $1.9 billion); China reporting an increase of 71.0 percent (to $3.3 billion); and similarly, with taxpayers in Hong Kong reporting an increase of 41.2 percent (to $2.9 billion).

European-based U.S. taxpayers reported the second largest amount of foreign-earned income of just under $14.4 billion, which was a real decrease of 3.2 percent from 2006. As in previous years, the United Kingdom continued to lead all countries from all continents with over $5.4 billion in foreign-earned income, accounting for more than a third of all European-based returns. This was a 22.1-percent decrease from $7.0 billion in 2006, contributing largely to the overall decrease from European-based returns.

Total foreign-earned income reported for North American-based taxpayers grew 22.9 percent for 2011. Canadian-based taxpayers drove this growth, reporting over $3.8 billion in foreign-earned income for the year, a 28.9-percent increase from 2006. Over 60 percent of all taxpayers reporting foreign-earned income had no U.S. income tax liability for 2011.

Foreign Tax Credit Highlights

From 2006 to 2011, inflation-adjusted foreign-source gross income reported on Form 1116, *Foreign Tax Credit*, grew 27.0 percent, and real foreign tax credits claimed rose 34.5 percent. U.S. taxpayers claimed a total of nearly $16.5 billion in foreign tax credits from approximately 6.9 million returns for 2011; these credits were based on a reported $170.0 billion in foreign-source gross income and $22.0 billion in foreign taxes paid or accrued.

As with foreign-earned income by country, the United Kingdom continued to lead in terms of foreign-source gross income reported on Form 1116. For 2011, taxpayers reported $13.9 billion in foreign-source gross income from the United Kingdom, a modest growth of 4.2 percent from the inflation-adjusted $13.3 billion reported for 2006. By region, taxpayers reported the most foreign-source gross income ($32.4 billion) from European countries for 2011. For the most significant regions, the Oceania countries (Australia, New Zealand, etc.) reported the largest growth. From 2006 to 2011, foreign-source gross income reported for these countries doubled to $2.7 billion, and the 113.9-percent growth from Australia contributed to most of this growth.

Overview of Foreign-Earned Income Provisions

In an effort to increase U.S. participation in foreign trade, a Federal income tax law was passed in 1926, which allowed for an exclusion of foreign-earned income from taxes. Under the 2011 version of the law, Section 911 of the Internal Revenue Code, qualified U.S. citizens or resident aliens living and working abroad could elect to exclude a certain amount of foreign-earned income and an excess foreign housing cost. The election was made separately for each of the exclusions. To qualify, an individual must have had a foreign tax home and satisfied either the bona fide residence or physical presence test. Only U.S. citizens could use the bona fide residence test. The bona fide residence test was generally satisfied if the individual had established and maintained a residence in a foreign country for an uninterrupted period that included an entire taxable year. An individual would not be considered a resident if a statement was submitted to the taxing authorities of the foreign country indicating nonresidency and the foreign country did not subject the individual to foreign income taxation. Under the physical presence test, an individual had to be present in a foreign country for at least 330 full days during any period of 12 consecutive months.

In general, earned income was compensation received for personal services. Thus, wages, salaries, and professional fees qualified as earned income for purposes of the exclusion. Taxpayers engaged in a trade or business that used both capital and services to produce income, could treat any reasonable amount that did not exceed 30 percent of the taxpayer's share of the net profits of the trade or business as earned income. Earned income also included employer-provided allowances or reimbursements, such as cost-of-living allowances, overseas compensation differentials, quarters, education allowances, and the full rental value of property or facilities provided by the employer. To qualify for the exclusions, the earned income had to be foreign-earned income.

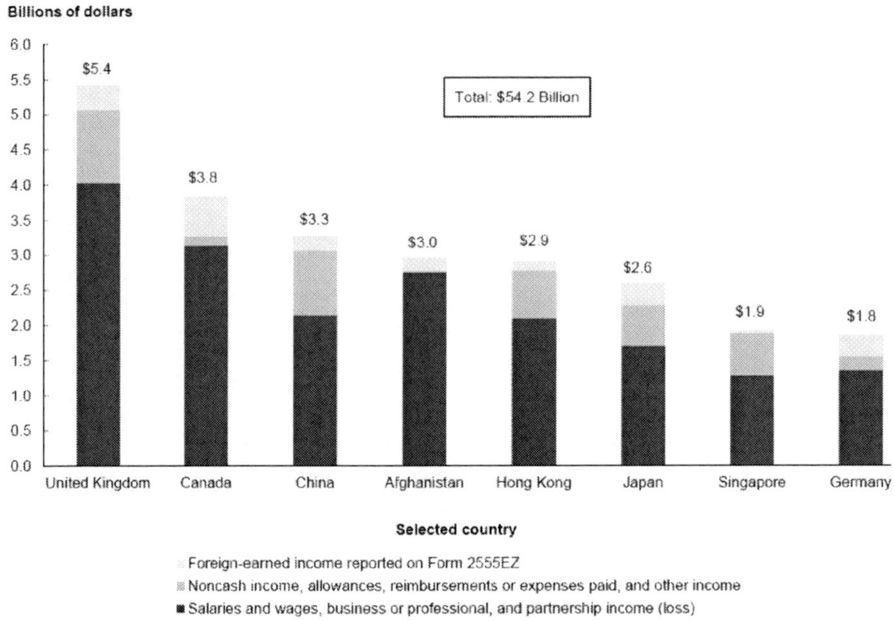

Note: Detail may not add to totals because of rounding. Data are from Forms 2555, Foreign Earned Income, filed by U.S. taxpayers with Form 1040, U.S. Individual Income Tax Return.

Source: IRS, Statistics of Income Division, Individual Foreign-Earned Income and Foreign Tax Credit, April 2014.

Figure A. Foreign-Earned Income by Selected Country, Tax Year 2011.

In general, it would be foreign-earned income if the taxpayer performed personal services in a foreign country. The actual location of the employer and employee at the time the taxpayer received the compensation did not affect this determination. Not included in foreign-earned income were pensions, annuities, compensation by the U.S. Government, and income excluded by an employer to compensate for meals and lodging provided for the employer's convenience.

For 2011, the maximum amount of foreign-earned income a taxpayer could exclude was $92,900, prorated on a daily basis for the qualifying period. (For 2006, this amount was $82,400.) If a taxpayer elected both the foreign-earned income and housing exclusions, the foreign housing exclusion was calculated first. The foreign-earned income exclusion was then limited to the excess of foreign-earned income over the housing exclusion.

Qualified housing expenses were reasonable housing costs paid or incurred during the tax year. In general, these expenses included utilities, insurance, and rent. The excess-housing cost was equal to the individual's qualified housing expenses for the tax year over a base-level amount ($14,864 for 2011) prorated on a daily basis. To the extent these were employer-provided amounts, the excess housing cost was allowed as a foreign housing exclusion. Housing costs related to self-employment were allowed as a foreign housing deduction in computing adjusted gross income. The foreign housing deduction was limited to the excess of foreign-earned income over the sum of foreign-earned income and housing exclusions. Any excess housing amount that was not deductible could be carried over to the following tax year.

In addition to the exclusions (foreign-earned income and housing) and the housing deduction, individuals could also claim a foreign tax credit (discussed in more detail in the Foreign Tax Credit Overview section). This credit was for foreign income taxes paid or accrued on two types of income: (1) foreign-earned income for which the income exclusion was not claimed, and (2) foreign-source income that did not qualify for the exclusions or deduction.

U.S. taxpayers file Form 2555, *Foreign Earned Income*, with Form 1040, *U.S. Individual Income Tax Return*, to claim the exclusions and the housing deduction.

For 2011, of the 145.4 million individual income tax returns filed with the Internal Revenue Service, an estimated 449,277 had a Form 2555 attached (or Form 2555- EZ), slightly more than 0.3 percent of the total.[1] Tables 1 and 2 present statistics for individual income tax returns with the foreign-earned income exclusion, foreign housing exclusion, and foreign housing deduction.

TOTAL FOREIGN-EARNED INCOME

For 2011, U.S. taxpayers reported $54.2 billion in foreign-earned income, a real increase of 32.3 percent from the 2006 inflation-adjusted amount of $41.0 billion. This represents a real annual growth rate of 5.8 percent from 2006.[2,3] This can be attributed to an increase in the number of returns filed with the exclusion, despite a decrease in the average amount of foreign-earned income reported per return. From 2006 to 2011, taxpayers filed approximately 115,000 more returns with the exclusion (up 34.2 percent). During this same period, the average amount of total foreign-earned income per return decreased approximately 1.4 percent in real terms, from an average of $122,424 for 2006 to $120,738 for 2011.

Of the nearly 450,000 returns filed with a Form 2555 attached, returns with a tax home of Canada (10.2 percent), the United Kingdom (7.0 percent), Japan (5.1 percent), Afghanistan (5.1 percent), and China (5.0 percent) represented about a third of the total number of returns filed for the year. In 2011, nearly 23,000 taxpayers reported a tax home of Afghanistan, a 288.2-percent increase from just under 6,000 taxpayers for 2006. The number of returns reporting China as a tax home grew steadily, rising 143.6 percent between 2001 and 2006, and another 79.6 percent between 2006 and 2011 (to over 22,000 returns). The large growth in Afghanistan, the continued growth in China, and the more modest increases in the number of returns from other tax homes in Asia, led to an overall 40.3-percent increase in Asian-based returns (Figure B). For 2011, the number of Asian-based returns with foreign-earned income (about 195,000) was nearly 82 percent higher than the number of returns for Europe (just over 107,000). These data show a decade of strong growth in Asian-based U.S. taxpayers since 2001, when Europe represented the region with the largest number of returns reported.

Along with the number of returns, U.S. taxpayers in Asian-based countries reported the largest increases in total earned income for 2011 (just over $24.9 billion), an increase of 52.2 percent from the amount reported for 2006. North American-based countries (up 22.9 percent) and Oceania countries (up 83.4 percent) also showed signißcant real increases. The latter occurred primarily due to returns from Australia nearly doubling the amount of foreign-earned income reported to $1.4 billion.

While the number of returns from Europe increased by 7.5 percent from 2006 to 2011, total foreign-earned income decreased 3.2 percent, in real dollars, to $14.4 billion. Decreases reported by taxpayers in the United Kingdom (down 22.1 percent) and Germany (down 3.9 percent) contributed to this decline. In contrast, foreign-earned income reported on returns from Latin/ South American-based countries increased 35.2 percent to nearly $1.8 billion during this same period. This reversed the loss reported in the previous study, when these countries reported a 16.7-percent decline in foreign-earned income from 2001.[4]

Figure B. Foreign-Earned Income, Exclusions, and Housing Deduction, by Selected Country or Region, Tax Years 2006 and 2011

[Money amounts are in thousands of dollars].

Selected country or region	Number of returns [1]			Total foreign-earned income			Foreign-earned income exclusion before deductions		
	2006 [2]	2011	Percentage change	2006 [2]	2011	Percentage change	2006 [2]	2011	Percentage change
	(1)	(2)	(3)	(4)	(5)	(6)	(7)	(8)	(9)
All geographic areas	334,851	449,277	34.2	40,993,722	54,244,646	32.3	20,483,374	28,344,312	38.4
North America	36,179	52,883	46.2	3,624,815	4,455,934	22.9	1,984,349	2,938,301	48.1
Canada	30,067	45,949	52.8	2,981,436	3,841,763	28.9	1,628,789	2,580,459	58.4
Other North America	6,112	6,934	13.4	643,379	614,171	-4.5	355,560	357,842	0.6
Asia	138,795	194,703	40.3	16,371,651	24,911,137	52.2	8,840,231	12,730,672	44.0
Afghanistan	5,912	22,951	288.2	496,232	2,961,433	496.8	368,102	1,749,519	375.3
China	12,430	22,328	79.6	1,910,958	3,267,117	71.0	828,647	1,444,917	74.4
Hong Kong	10,792	13,181	22.1	2,058,484	2,905,841	41.2	768,852	975,487	26.9
Iraq	18,325	14,021	-23.5	2,039,515	1,552,010	-23.9	1,325,470	1,029,197	-22.4
Israel	8,986	9,872	9.9	564,748	645,902	14.4	448,417	488,073	8.8
Japan	23,529	23,054	-2.0	2,350,711	2,593,308	10.3	1,244,670	1,246,605	0.2
Saudi Arabia	5,109	7,968	56.0	688,662	1,135,434	64.9	407,436	598,546	46.9
Singapore	3,636	7,749	113.1	834,525	1,914,293	129.4	291,687	634,166	117.4
South Korea	6,668	13,659	104.8	774,384	1,123,230	45.0	390,366	656,363	68.1
United Arab Emirates	7,423	12,153	63.7	847,611	1,623,109	91.5	563,940	905,731	60.6
Other Asia	35,988	47,769	32.7	3,805,820	5,189,461	36.4	2,202,642	3,002,067	36.3
Europe	99,732	107,220	7.5	14,848,191	14,367,774	-3.2	6,119,048	6,668,589	9.0
France	9,653	11,111	15.1	1,054,319	1,209,808	14.7	552,329	623,621	12.9

Figure B. (Continued)

Selected country or region	Number of returns [1]			Total foreign-earned income			Foreign-earned income exclusion before deductions		
	2006 [2]	2011	Percentage change	2006 [2]	2011	Percentage change	2006 [2]	2011	Percentage change
Germany	21,513	19,173	-10.9	1,917,976	1,843,857	-3.9	1,171,725	1,101,969	-6.0
Switzerland	7,093	10,548	48.7	1,113,016	1,832,500	64.6	512,414	834,680	62.9
United Kingdom	28,409	31,599	11.2	6,961,514	5,421,593	-22.1	1,925,680	1,944,761	1.0
Other Europe	33,067	34,790	5.2	3,801,365	4,060,017	6.8	1,956,900	2,163,558	10.6
Latin/South America	13,911	14,732	5.9	1,299,931	1,757,461	35.2	755,500	880,165	16.5
Oceania	9,724	14,449	48.6	950,171	1,742,935	83.4	598,599	954,874	59.5
Australia	6,420	10,353	61.3	738,594	1,443,738	95.5	432,200	707,197	63.6
Other Oceania	3,305	4,097	24.0	211,577	299,197	41.4	166,398	247,676	48.8
Other	36,510	65,290	78.8	3,898,963	7,009,404	79.8	2,185,647	4,171,712	90.9

Selected country or region	Housing exclusion			Housing deduction		
	2006 [2]	2011	Percentage change	2006 [2]	2011	Percentage change
	(10)	(11)	(12)	(13)	(14)	(15)
All geographic areas	**1,491,218**	**1,578,263**	**5.8**	**93,318**	**99,010**	**6.1**
North America	**30,841**	**22,816**	**-26.0**	**530**	**1,949**	**267.7**
Canada	13,239	14,766	11.5	* 176	1,789	914.7
Other North America	17,602	8,049	-54.3	* 355	* 160	-54.9
Asia	**719,693**	**923,406**	**28.3**	**43,143**	**47,189**	**9.4**
Afghanistan	0	3,220	[3]	* 125	* 254	103.2
China	125,439	137,003	9.2	3,111	5,610	80.3

Selected country or region	Housing exclusion			Housing deduction		
	2006 [2]	2011	Percentage change	2006 [2]	2011	Percentage change
Hong Kong	217,393	232,093	6.8	14,946	11,677	-21.9
Iraq	2,555	2,757	7.9	* 925	* 150	-83.8
Israel	725	2,515	246.8	162	* 146	-9.8
Japan	149,320	141,647	-5.1	11,313	13,963	23.4
Saudi Arabia	7,088	9,095	28.3	* 4	980	[3]
Singapore	58,831	153,308	160.6	762	3,123	309.8
South Korea	43,359	33,895	-21.8	3,321	1,764	-46.9
United Arab Emirates	30,384	89,278	193.8	3,615	5,738	58.7
Other Asia	84,598	118,596	40.2	4,862	3,783	-22.2
Europe	**607,948**	**447,264**	**-26.4**	**42,000**	**35,879**	**-14.6**
France	43,196	53,453	23.7	4,232	4,229	-0.1
Germany	57,232	50,701	-11.4	3,861	5,704	47.7
Switzerland	55,100	69,010	25.2	1,637	3,245	98.2
United Kingdom	330,915	153,213	-53.7	24,909	17,090	-31.4
Other Europe	121,506	120,890	-0.5	7,362	5,611	-23.8
Latin/South America	**33,548**	**31,846**	**-5.1**	**969**	**2,577**	**166.1**
Oceania	**13,326**	**34,444**	**158.5**	*** 55**	**556**	**916.9**
Australia	12,809	32,469	153.5	* 54	441	723.4
Other Oceania	519	1,975	280.6	* 1	* 115	[3]
Other	**85,861**	**118,488**	**38.0**	**6,621**	**10,861**	**64.0**

* Estimate should be used with caution because of the small number of sample returns on which it is based.

[1] Data are from Forms 2555, *Foreign Earned Income,* filed by U.S. taxpayers with Form 1040, *U.S. Individual Income Tax Return.*

[2] For comparability, 2006 amounts have been adjusted for inflation to 2011 constant dollars. The inflation-adjusted constant dollars are based on the Consumer Price Index (CPI-U) computed and reported by the U.S. Department of Labor, Bureau of Labor

Statistics, *Monthly Labor Review.* The consumer price index represents annual averages of monthly indices and approximates buying patterns of typical urban consumers.

Year	CPI-U
2011	224.939
2006	201.600

Percentage not computed.

NOTE: Detail may not add to totals because of rounding.

Source: IRS, Statistics of Income Division, Individual Foreign-Earned Income and Foreign Tax Credit, April 2014.

As in previous years, United Kingdom-based individuals reported the largest amount of foreign-earned income (just over $5.4 billion) in 2011. However, the decline for these taxpayers (down 22.1 percent), along with rapid growth in several other countries, reduced the overall share of foreign-earned income in the United Kingdom from 17.0 percent for 2006 to 10.0 percent for 2011. The difference in total foreign-earned income between the United Kingdom (the largest source) and Canada (the second largest source) was $1.6 billion. For 2006, the gap in total foreign-earned income reported on returns from these two countries was approximately $4.0 billion.

China-based U.S. taxpayers continued to report remarkable growth in total foreign-earned income. For these taxpayers, total foreign-earned income grew 71.0 percent, in real terms, from approximately $1.9 billion for 2006 to nearly $3.3 billion for 2011. Other Asia-based returns, United Arab Emirates (up 91.5 percent to $1.6 billion) and Saudi Arabia (up 64.9 percent to $1.1 billion), also showed large increases during this same period.

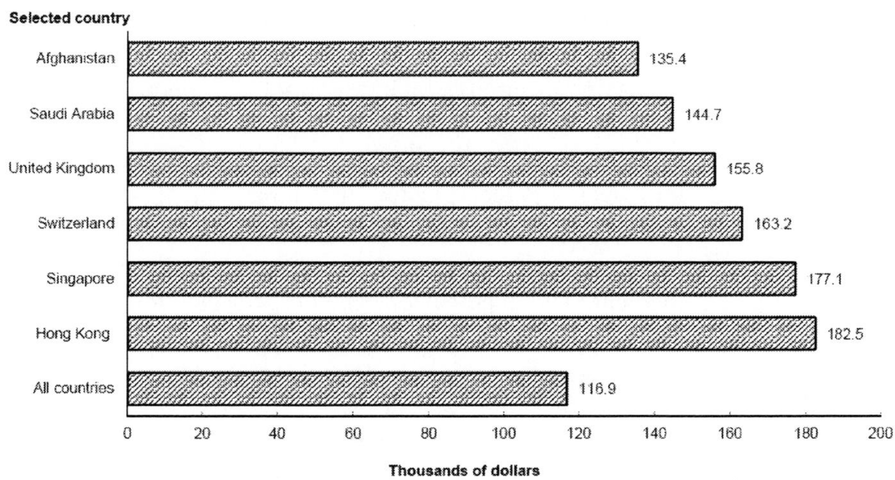

Note: U.S. taxpayers filed Form 2555, *Foreign Earned Income*, with Form 1040, *U.S. Individual Income Tax Return*.

Source: IRS, Statistics of Income Division, Individual Foreign-Earned Income and Foreign Tax Credit, April 2014.

Figure C. Average Foreign Salaries and Wages Earned by U.S. Taxpayers Reporting Wages on Form 2555, by Selected Country, Tax Year 2011.

Individuals with tax homes in the United Kingdom (10.0 percent), Canada (7.1 percent), China (6.0 percent), Afghanistan (5.5 percent), Hong Kong (5.4

percent), Japan (4.8 percent), Singapore (3.5 percent), and Germany (3.4 percent) accounted for approximately 45.6 percent of the total foreign-earned income for 2011 (Figure A). Of these selected countries, six also had the largest amounts of income for the 2006 study, with Afghanistan and Singapore replacing Iraq and Switzerland for 2011. In rank order, China jumped from the seventh to the third highest amount of foreign-earned income, while Afghanistan took the fourth spot. The only other movement for these countries from the 2006 study was Hong Kong moving ahead of Japan. While foreign-earned income decreased in the United Kingdom (down 22.1 percent) and Germany (down 3.9 percent), it increased in the six remaining countries.

Composition of Foreign-Earned Income

For 2011, of the $54.2 billion in foreign-earned income (cited above), taxpayers reported just under $49.2 billion on Form 2555. Taxpayers reported the remaining $5.1 billion using Form 2555-EZ. Data related to the composition of foreign-earned income are not available on Form 2555-EZ; therefore, the breakdown in the ensuing discussion includes only those amounts reported on Form 2555.

Salaries and wages comprised 76.7 percent of the total foreign-earned income reported for 2011 (Table 1). Of the remaining 23.3 percent, allowances, reimbursements, or expenses paid by employers made up 10.6 percent; business or professional, and partnership, noncash and other income accounted for 12.7 percent. The average foreign-source salary for a taxpayer ßling Form 2555 (with wages) was approximately $116,858. This average, however, varied greatly among the various countries. Of the top six countries, (those with the highest average wages with at least 5,000 Forms 2555 attached to individual tax returns); returns from Hong Kong-based taxpayers reported the highest average salary ($182,500) for 2011, followed by Singapore ($177,059). Afghanistan reported the lowest average salary ($135,412) (Figure C).

The average salary reported for Hong Kong returns increased by just over $23,000 (in real dollars) from 2006. Also, for 2011, the difference in average salary between Hong Kong and Singapore was just over $5,400. In comparison, for the 2006 study, the United Kingdom and Hong Kong were the top two countries, respectively, based on average salary. At that time, the average salary reported by taxpayers based in the United Kingdom was approximately $32,000 higher than the average salary earned in Hong Kong.

FOREIGN-EARNED INCOME EXCLUSION, HOUSING EXCLUSION, AND HOUSING DEDUCTION

From 2006 to 2011, the total amount reported for the foreign-earned income exclusion grew 38.4 percent (in real terms) to $28.3 billion. This growth occurred while the amount of foreign-earned income that a taxpayer could exclude increased from $82,400 to $92,900. The amount reported for the housing exclusion increased approximately 5.8 percent, from an inflation-adjusted $1.5 billion to $1.6 billion. The housing deduction also increased in real terms (6.1 percent), to a total of $99.0 million for 2011.

Increases in both the housing exclusion and housing deduction can mostly be attributed to more taxpayers claiming these benefits. Also, some of this growth may be due to higher limits placed on the amount of housing expenses eligible for the exclusion or deduction. In general, a limit of $27,870 (up from $24,720 in 2006) was placed on eligible housing expenses; however, taxpayers could take a higher expense amount if they resided in specific countries or cities listed by the IRS in the instructions for Form 2555, *Foreign Earned Income.*

For 2011, individuals with a tax home of Canada reported the highest amount of exclusions for foreign-earned income, followed by the United Kingdom and Afghanistan. Canadian-based taxpayers reported $2.6 billion in foreign-earned income exclusions for the year, up 58.4 percent from the inflation-adjusted $1.6 billion excluded in 2006. In comparison, United Kingdom-based taxpayers reported over $1.9 billion, up 1.0 percent from 2006, despite the 22.1-percent decline in reported foreign-earned income cited above. Afghanistan reported over $1.7 billion in foreign-earned income exclusions, after only reporting $0.4 billion for 2006. The 375.3-percent growth in Afghanistan, coupled with a 74.4-percent increase in China (to over $1.4 billion), contributed to much of the overall 44.0-percent growth in foreign-earned income from Asian-based taxpayers for 2011.

Of the $1.6 billion reported for 2011 (cited above), individuals with a tax home of Hong Kong (14.7 percent), the United Kingdom (9.7 percent), Japan (9.0 percent) or China (8.7 percent) accounted for about 42.1 percent of the housing exclusion reported for the year. This overall increase reversed the 38.7-percent decrease reported in the 2006 study.

Taxpayers with foreign-earned income use the housing deduction to increase their total statutory adjustments, thus decreasing their adjusted gross income. For 2011, just over 5,500 taxpayers claimed the housing deduction for a total of $99.0 million. The average housing deduction was $17,763 for the year.

Individual taxpayers claiming both the foreign-earned income and housing exclusions, along with the housing deduction, reported worldwide income of over $73.4 billion for 2011. After claiming the exclusions and deduction, these taxpayers reduced their worldwide income by $30.0 billion, or almost 41 percent. Approximately 60.8 percent of all taxpayers who claimed the exclusions, deduction, and any foreign tax credit to which they were entitled, had no U.S. income tax liability for 2011. This was up from 57.4 percent from 2006.

Starting in 2006, individual taxpayers reporting foreign-earned income used a new foreign-earned income tax worksheet to figure out their tax, and to calculate the tax on nonexcluded income using tax rates that would have applied had they not claimed the exclusion. For 2011, the change in the calculation affected just over 210,000 returns, resulting in an additional $1.4 billion in tax. In comparison, this change affected nearly 139,000 returns for 2006, resulting in an additional $0.8 billion in tax.

Overview of Foreign Tax Credit Provisions

For 2011, U.S. taxpayers with income from sources outside the United States, regardless of their residency, could claim a credit against their U.S. income tax liabilities for most foreign taxes paid or accrued (except for taxes paid on income excluded under the foreign-earned income provisions). The purpose of the credit, originally created in 1918, is to avoid double taxation on foreign-source income, since the United States taxes its citizens and resident aliens based on their worldwide incomes.

The foreign tax credit is subject to a limitation based on the taxpayer's total U.S. income tax liability. This prevents taxpayers from using foreign taxes paid in relatively high-tax-rate countries from offsetting taxes paid on their U.S.-source incomes. The limitation is computed separately for the following categories of foreign-source income: passive income, general income, Section 901(j) income, certain income re-sourced by a treaty, and lump-sum distributions from certain retirement plans. The allowable credits for each category of foreign-source income are then added together.

Passive income generally includes dividends, interest, rents, royalties, and annuities. Section 901(j) income is income earned from activities conducted in a sanctioned country; no credit is allowed for taxes paid or accrued to sanctioned countries.[5] Certain income re-sourced by treaty allows specific types of income to be treated as foreign-source income, if there is a tax treaty that treats it as such, and the treaty is applied. Lump-sum distributions are distributions from a retirement plan that are subject to U.S. tax using income averaging. General income is foreign income from sources outside the United States that do not fall into one of the other four categories; it includes high-taxed income that would otherwise be passive income.

In general, for taxpayers who file Form 1116, *Foreign Tax Credit*, with Form 1040, the limitation on the foreign tax credit for each type of income is calculated by multiplying the total U.S. income tax liability before credits by the ratio of the foreign-source taxable income for that type of income to total U.S. taxable income.[6] However, not all taxpayers who claim the foreign tax credit file Form 1116 (see Data Sources and Limitations). Foreign taxes paid in excess of the limitation can be carried back 1 year and then forward for up to 10 years. Taxes carried to another year are added to the taxes available for credit for that year for the same income category. Tables 3 through 5 present statistics on the foreign tax credit and related foreign-source income reported on individual income tax returns.

Figure D. Selected Income and Credit Items, Tax Years 2006 and 2011
[Money amounts are in thousands of dollars]

Item	2006 [1]	2011	Percentage change
Worldwide income, all 1040 returns (2]	(1)	(2)	(3)
	9,109,773,918	**8,528,125,741**	**-6.4**
Worldwide income, returns with Form 1116 (3]	**1,330,969,514**	**1,155,322,207**	**-13.2**
Form 1116			
Foreign-source gross income	133,857,682	169,982,715	27.0
Foreign tax credit [4]	12,227,706	16,451,088	34.5

[1] For comparability, 2006 amounts have been adjusted for inflation to 2011 constant dollars. The inflation-adjusted constant dollars are based on the Consumer Price Index (CPI-U) computed and reported by the U.S. Department of Labor, Bureau of Labor Statistics, *Monthly Labor Review.* The consumer price index represents annual averages of monthly indices and approximates buying patterns of typical urban consumers.

Year	CPI-U
2011	224.939
2006	201.6

[2] Worldwide income is total income or loss reported on Form 1040 before the foreign-earned income and housing exclusions have been taken.
[3] U.S. taxpayers file Form 1116, *Foreign Tax Credit,* with Form 1040, *U.S. Individual Income Tax Return,* per the instructions for Form 1116 (see www.irs.gov/form 1116).
[4] Includes foreign tax credits reported on Form 1040 without a supporting Form 1116. Taxpayers with $300 ($600 if married filing a joint return) or less in creditable foreign taxes who also meet certain other conditions are not required to file Form 1116 to claim the foreign tax credit. Source: IRS, Statistics of Income Division, Individual Foreign-Earned Income and Foreign Tax Credit, April 2014.

FOREIGN-SOURCE GROSS INCOME

Foreign-source gross income is all income earned outside the United States, except for income used to claim the foreign-earned income exclusion. Taxpayers reported just under $170.0 billion in foreign-source gross income for 2011 (Figure D). This represents approximately 14.7 percent of total worldwide income for those taxpayers who reported foreign-source gross income and 2.0 percent of total worldwide income for all U.S. taxpayers. These statistics include only foreign-source gross income reported on Form 1116, because some taxpayers with this type of income do not file this form.[7] Between 2006 and 2011, foreign-source gross income grew 27.0 percent in real percentage terms, whereas worldwide income reported on all individual U.S. tax returns fell 6.4 percent.

Of the nearly $170.0 billion in foreign-source gross income, taxpayers reported $87.6 billion (or 51.5 percent) without stating a specific country, and the remaining $82.4 billion stated a specific country.[8] The United Kingdom ($13.9 billion), followed by Canada ($12.9 billion), Germany ($5.6 billion), Colombia ($4.3 billion), and China ($3.9 billion) made up the top five countries with the most foreign-source income. Of these, all but China was in the top five for 2006. China surpassed Japan in this category for 2011.

Together, the top five countries accounted for about half (49.3 percent) of all foreign-source gross income with a stated country. Of this percentage, taxpayers reported earning 16.9 percent from the United Kingdom, followed by Canada (15.7 percent), Germany (6.7 percent), Colombia (5.2 percent), and China (4.8 percent) (Figure E).

U.S. taxpayers filing Form 1116 reported earning an average of $47,522 in foreign-source gross income for 2011. For the top five countries, taxpayers reported the highest average foreign-source gross income for Colombia

($1,244,965), followed by China ($162,219), the United Kingdom ($133,849), Germany ($124,558), and Canada ($40,442) (Figure F).

Among the geographic regions with the most significant foreign-source gross income, Oceania had the highest growth between 2006 and 2011. For this region, foreign-source gross income grew 100.9 percent, rising to just under $2.7 billion for 2011, from an inflation-adjusted $1.3 billion for 2006. Much of this increase was due to the growth in Australia, up 113.9 percent from $1.1 billion for 2006 to $2.4 billion for 2011.

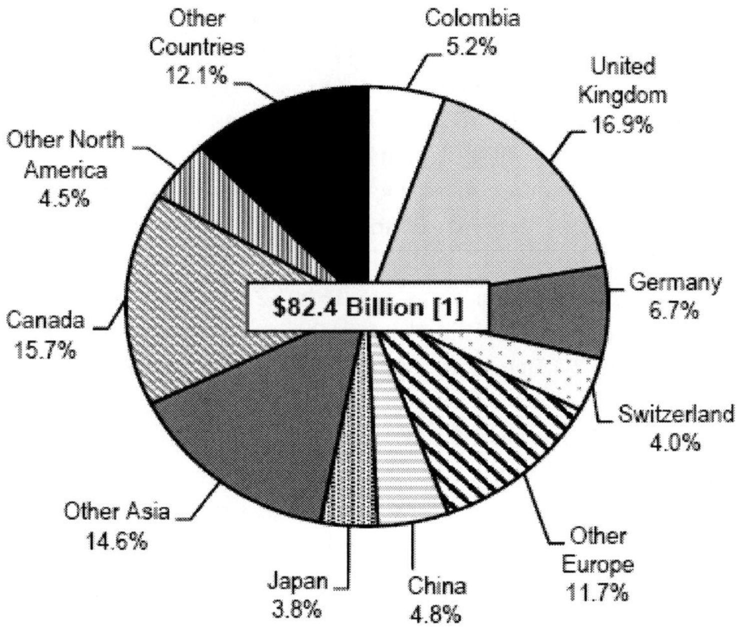

[1] Foreign-source gross income reported on the Form 1116, Foreign Tax Credit, with stated country or region. Total foreign-source gross income (including that reported without a country or region) was $170.0 billion.

Note: Percentages may not add to 100 due to rounding.

Source: IRS, Statistics of Income Division, Individual Foreign-Earned Income and Foreign Tax Credit, April 2014.

Figure E. Foreign-Source Gross Income, by Selected Country or Region, Tax Year 2011.

Despite the large growth for Oceania countries, the amount of foreign-source gross income ($2.7 billion) was still much smaller than for other regions. Europe had the largest foreign-source gross income ($32.4 billion), yet the percentage growth for this region (16.9 percent) between 2006 and 2011 was the smallest. Asia had the second largest amount of foreign-source gross income ($19.1 billion), followed by North America ($16.7 billion). For additional data on foreign-source gross income by region or country, see Table 4.

FOREIGN TAXES AND FOREIGN TAX CREDIT

For 2011, U.S. taxpayers paid (or accrued) $22.0 billion in foreign taxes as reported on Form 1116. This was before carrybacks, carryovers, reductions, and reclassifications. The United Kingdom, Canada, Germany, China, and Switzerland made up the top five countries in terms of foreign taxes paid or accrued and accounted for 44.4 percent of the total.

Similar to foreign-source gross income, the highest amount ($4.4 billion) and greatest share (25.8 percent) of total foreign taxes paid or accrued to a stated country was for the United Kingdom. Canada was the next largest recipient of foreign taxes paid or accrued ($2.4 billion or 14.0 percent), followed by Germany ($1.1 billion or 6.1 percent), China (nearly $1.0 billion or 5.7 percent), and Switzerland ($0.9 billion or 5.1 percent). Of the $22.0 billion in foreign taxes paid or accrued, taxpayers reported $4.8 billion (approximately 21.8 percent of the total amount) without a stated country (Figure G).[9]

Total foreign taxes paid or accrued grew 42.3 percent between 2006 and 2011. Among the most significant regions, Oceania had the highest growth (126.3 percent). This was primarily due to the 131.0-percent real growth in foreign taxes paid or accrued to Australia. Latin/South America showed the next highest growth (103.9 percent). Even with this large growth, however, the amount paid or accrued to Oceania and Latin/South America countries (about $0.65 billion each) was still small compared to Europe, Asia, and North America, the three largest regions in terms of foreign taxes paid. Of these regions, Asia grew the most (59.4 percent), followed by Europe (37.2 percent) and North America (22.4 percent) in terms of foreign taxes paid or accrued.

Collectively, European countries made up the largest recipient of foreign taxes paid or accrued ($8.3 billion), and the United Kingdom accounted for over half ($4.4 billion) of this amount. In addition, foreign taxes paid or accrued to European countries was nearly twice as high as Asian countries ($4.2 billion), the next highest region.

Figure F. Foreign-Source Gross Income and Foreign Taxes, by Selected Country or Region, Tax Years 2006 and 2011
[Money amounts are in thousands of dollars]

Item, selected country or region	2006 [1]		2011		Percentage change in amount
	Number of returns [2]	Amount	Number of returns [2]	Amount	
	(1)	(2)	(3)	(4)	(5)
Foreign-source gross income, total	**2,789,011**	**133,857,682**	**3,576,909**	**169,982,715**	**27.0**
North America	**227,240**	**13,538,418**	**336,594**	**16,652,533**	**23.0**
Canada	212,857	11,120,480	319,821	12,934,181	16.3
Other North America	16,723	2,417,937	29,071	3,718,353	53.8
Asia	**102,977**	**13,051,307**	**140,980**	**19,093,930**	**46.3**
China	14,079	1,761,713	24,258	3,935,103	123.4
Hong Kong	7,306	1,767,011	8,578	2,660,033	50.5
Japan	34,876	2,897,434	35,140	3,115,052	7.5
Other Asia	58,486	6,625,150	78,459	9,383,744	41.6
Europe	**277,003**	**27,683,076**	**291,596**	**32,365,839**	**16.9**
Germany	38,839	4,175,696	44,614	5,557,019	33.1
Switzerland	19,591	1,527,427	18,273	3,299,242	116.0
United Kingdom	104,193	13,323,192	103,755	13,887,534	4.2
Other Europe	146,479	8,656,761	142,586	9,622,041	11.2
Latin/South America	**14,554**	**4,832,364**	**26,997**	**7,202,573**	**49.0**
Colombia	1,233	3,585,999	3,467	4,316,293	20.4
Other Latin/South America	14,867	1,246,366	23,975	2,886,280	131.6
Oceania	**14,434**	**1,335,292**	**22,867**	**2,682,217**	**100.9**
Australia	10,373	1,120,991	16,929	2,398,005	113.9
Other Oceania	4,225	214,300	6,140	284,213	32.6
Other	**42,561**	**3,055,492**	**43,331**	**4,395,318**	**43.8**
Country not stated (3]	**2,288,708**	**70,361,733**	**2,972,191**	**87,590,305**	**24.5**
Foreign taxes paid or accrued, total	**2,648,572**	**15,493,433**	**3,366,548**	**22,039,411**	**42.3**
North America	**215,827**	**2,270,168**	**316,829**	**2,778,640**	**22.4**
Canada	201,280	1,978,872	296,762	2,414,016	22.0
Other North America	15,132	291,297	23,392	364,624	25.2
Asia	**90,063**	**2,620,337**	**133,848**	**4,177,757**	**59.4**
China	12,165	524,033	21,861	981,874	87.4
Hong Kong	5,960	302,276	7,715	395,809	30.9
Japan	29,902	734,963	34,504	861,206	17.2
Other Asia	50,056	1,059,065	73,138	1,938,866	83.1
Europe	**246,302**	**6,052,802**	**264,856**	**8,305,468**	**37.2**
Germany	35,194	848,231	42,952	1,058,811	24.8

Figure F. (Continued)

Item, selected country or region	2006 [1]		2011		Percentage change in amount
	Number of returns [2]	Amount	Number of returns [2]	Amount	
Switzerland	18,262	434,353	16,692	880,575	102.7
United Kingdom	84,396	3,399,853	92,524	4,440,803	30.6
Other Europe	130,914	1,370,366	127,603	1,925,280	40.5
Latin/South America	**13,639**	**319,324**	**23,406**	**651,001**	**103.9**
Colombia	1,190	92,527	2,401	135,133	46.0
Other Latin/South America	13,165	226,796	21,279	515,869	127.5
Oceania	**11,620**	**285,084**	**20,897**	**645,055**	**126.3**
Australia	7,950	258,880	15,107	598,001	131.0
Other Oceania	3,801	26,203	5,921	47,054	79.6
Other	**37,266**	**397,396**	**34,608**	**678,629**	**70.8**
Country not stated (4)	**2,175,744**	**3,548,317**	**2,751,865**	**4,802,859**	**35.4**

[1] For comparability, 2006 amounts have been adjusted for inflation to 2011 constant dollars. The inflation-adjusted constant dollars are based on the Consumer Price Index (CPI-U)

computed and reported by the U.S. Department of Labor, Bureau of Labor Statistics, *Monthly Labor Review.*

Year CPI-U

2011 224.939

2006 201.6

[2] Number of returns detail does not add to total because taxpayers may report data for more than one country per return.

[3] For Tax Year 2011 the $87.6 billion of total foreign-source gross income reported without a specific country or region being stated include $0.1 billion for high-taxed income.

[4] For Tax Year 2011 the $4.8 billion of total foreign taxes paid or accrued reported without a specific country or region being stated include $4.3 million for high-taxed income. NOTES: Detail may not add to totals because of rounding. Data are from Forms 1116, *Foreign Tax Credit,* which U.S. taxpayers file with Form 1040, *U.S. Individual Income Tax Return.*

Source: IRS, Statistics of Income Division, Individual Foreign-Earned Income and Foreign Tax Credit, April 2014.

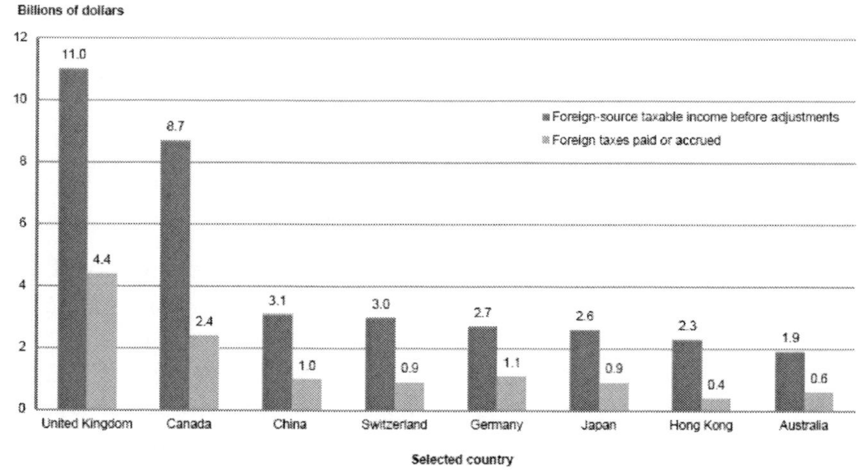

Source: IRS, Statistics of Income Division, Individual Foreign-Earned Income and Foreign Tax and Credit, April 2014.

Figure G. Foreign-Source Taxable Income and Foreign Taxes, by Selected Country, Tax Year 2011.

General limitation income, the income type for which most of the $22.0 billion in foreign taxes reported on Form 1116 was paid or accrued, accounted for nearly $18.1 billion in foreign taxes (82.0 percent of the total). Passive income was the next largest income type with just over $3.8 billion (17.4 percent of the total) in foreign taxes. Total foreign taxes available for credit after carry-backs, carryover, reductions, and reclassißcations under high-tax kickout[10] were $33.8 billion, and the foreign tax credit before adjustments (gross foreign tax credit) was approximately $16.2 billion (Table 3) (See Explanation of Selected Terms). Table 5 presents additional data on foreign taxes, by income type.

For 2011, taxpayers reported a foreign tax credit on 6.9 million individual tax returns, an increase of 7.6 percent from 6.4 million returns for 2006. The foreign tax credit grew 34.5 percent in real terms, rising $4.2 billion from the inÔation-adjusted $12.2 billion reported for 2006 to slightly under $16.5 billion for 2011.

Though the foreign tax credit grew between 2006 and 2011, it did not do so each year. For 2009, the total inÔation-adjusted foreign tax credits claimed fell 20.9 percent. For all other years, the foreign tax credit grew, rising 36.9 percent for 2007, followed by a 3.4-percent growth for 2008, a 14.7-percent growth for 2010, and a 4.8-percent growth for 2011. The average foreign tax credit for 2011 was $2,383, up from $1,905 (in 2011 constant dollars) for 2006 (Figure H).

SUMMARY

For 2011, the total amount of foreign-earned income reported by U.S. taxpayers grew 32.3 percent, in real terms, to over $54.2 billion. Returns from Asian-based countries realized the largest increase (in real dollars), rising by more than $8.5 billion, while North American-based countries (up $0.8 billion) and Oceania-based countries (also, up $0.8 billion) showed modest gains. Foreign-earned income in European-based countries declined 3.2 percent, after showing an increase of 10.2 percent during the 2006 study.

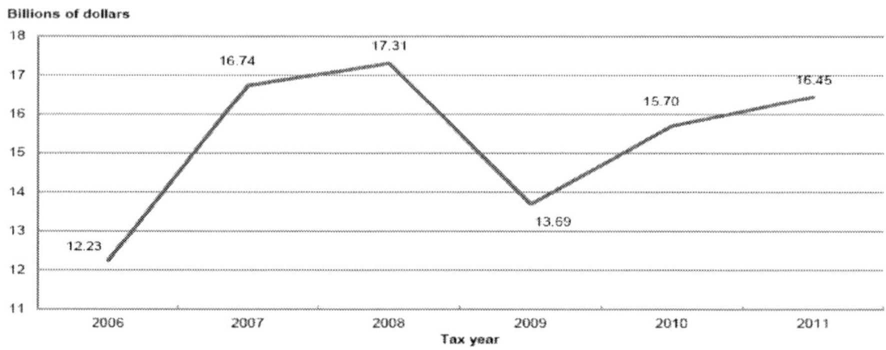

NOTES: For comparability, all amounts have been adjusted for inflation to 2011 constant dollars. The inflation-adjusted constant dollars are based on the Comsumer Price Index (CPI-U) computed and reported by the U.S. Department of Labor, Bureau of Labor Statistics, *Monthly Labor Review.*

Year	**CPI-U**
2011	224.939
2010	281.056
2009	214.537
2008	215.303
2007	207.342
2006	201.6

Data are from Forms 1116, *Foreign Tax Credit,* which U.S. taxpayers file with Form 1040, *U.S. Individual Income Tax Return.*

Source: IRS, Statistics of Income Division, Individual Foreign-Earned Income and Foreign Tax Credit, April 2014.

Figure H. Foreign Tax Credit, Tax Years 2006–2011.

While taxpayers with a tax home in the United Kingdom reported the most foreign-earned income (just over $5.4 billion), those in Afghanistan reported the largest overall growth, increasing 496.8 percent to just under $3.0 billion for 2011. U.S. taxpayers in Australia (up 95.5 percent), United Arab Emirates (up 91.5 percent), China (up 71.0 percent), and Saudi Arabia (up 64.9 percent) reported substantial growth in foreign-earned income. China-based ($3.3 billion) and Afghanistan-based ($3.0 billion) taxpayers reported the third and fourth highest amount of foreign-earned income. The total amount of housing exclusion claimed increased by 5.8 percent, from $1.5 billion reported for 2006 to $1.6 billion for 2011.

Foreign-source gross income reported by U.S. taxpayers reached nearly $170.0 billion for 2011, and the total foreign tax credit claimed was just under $16.5 billion. In real terms, this represents a 27.0-percent growth in foreign-source gross income and a 34.5-percent growth in the foreign tax credit from 2006, the last year a study was prepared on these data. As the source of $32.4 billion in foreign-source gross income and the recipient of $8.3 billion in foreign taxes paid, European countries were the largest component of these measures. The United Kingdom had the largest of these measures, with $13.9 billion in foreign-source gross income and $4.4 billion in foreign taxes paid. Additionally, taxpayers claimed a foreign tax credit on 6.9 million returns, an increase of just 7.6 percent from 2006, while the size of the credit grew 34.5 percent in real terms over this period.

Data Sources and Limitations

The IRS Statistics of Income Division (SOI) based the 2011 data presented in this article on a sample of individual income tax returns, Forms 1040, processed during Calendar Year 2012. These returns had one or more of the following: a foreign tax credit, an attached Form 1116, foreign-earned income exclusion, housing exclusion or housing deduction, or an attached Form 2555 or Form 2555-EZ. SOI understated the foreign-source income and taxes in this article to the extent that they either were not, or did not, have to be reported on Form 1116 to support the foreign tax credit claimed on Form 1040. Taxpayers with $300 ($600 if married filing a joint return) or less in creditable foreign taxes who also met certain other conditions were not required to file Form 1116 to claim the foreign tax credit. Therefore, about 60.0 percent of Forms 1040 (as originally filed) with a foreign tax credit did not include the supporting Form 1116. The average foreign tax credit reported on these returns was $69. Foreign-source income and losses are also understated to the extent that taxpayers who were not eligible for a credit did not file Form 1116. Taxpayers who had foreign-source income, but paid no taxes or had no U.S. tax liability before credits, could not claim a foreign tax credit.

Of the sampled returns, taxpayers filed about 1.8 percent with a foreign tax credit or an attached Form 1116, and 13.7 percent with an attached Form 2555 or Form 2555-EZ, on delinquent returns for tax years prior to 2011. Because these prior-year returns were processed during the 2011 filing period, SOI included them as a representation of 2011 returns filed after December 31, 2012. The sampled returns used for the statistics do not reflect adjustments made during audit examination, which determines the acceptability of the reported data.

SOI stratified the sample based on the: (1) presence or absence of Form 2555, *Foreign Earned Income,* Form 2555-EZ, *Foreign Earned Income Exclusion,* and Form 1116, *Foreign Tax Credit*; (2) presence or absence of other specific forms or schedules; (3) larger of positive income or negative income; (4) size of business and farm receipts; and (5) usefulness of returns for tax policy modeling purposes. The data from Form 2555, *Foreign Earned Income* and Form 1116, *Foreign Tax Credit,* for 2011 are based on a sample of 124,704 returns and a population of 8,372,358 returns. For a general description of the sampling procedures and data limitations of Statistics of Income tabulations, see *Statistics of Income, Individual Income Tax Returns 2011*, IRS Publication 1304, and the appendix to this issue of the *Bulletin.*

ADDITIONAL TABULAR DATA ON TAX STATS

For additional Form 2555 and Form 1116 data, see the Individual section of the Tax Stats Webpages at http:// www.irs.gov/uac/SOI-. This site includes data on foreign-earned income and the foreign tax credit, by form, tax years, country or region, type of income, and size of adjusted gross income. Since 1991, the IRS Statistics of Income (SOI) Division has published these data in 5-year intervals. *SOI Bulletin* articles are also available for 1996, 2001, and 2006.

EXPLANATION OF SELECTED TERMS

Definitions used in this article are generally the same as those in *Statistics of Income, Individual Income Tax Returns 2011,* IRS Publication 1304. The following is a partial list of definitions for terms that cannot be found in IRS Publication 1304.

Foreign Taxes Available for Credit—This is total foreign taxes paid or accrued plus carryovers, less reductions in foreign taxes, and adjusted for taxes reclassified under high-tax kickout.

Foreign-Tax-Credit Adjustments—These include reductions for participation in unsanctioned international boycotts and increases permitted by tax treaties between the United States and certain foreign countries.

Foreign-Source-Taxable Income—This is foreign-source gross income less deductions and losses.

The deductions include any expenses directly related to foreign-source income, a prorated share of the taxpayer's itemized or standard deductions, and a prorated share of interest expenses.

Gross-Foreign-Tax Credit—This is foreign tax credits before being limited to tax and before foreign tax credit adjustments are taken.

Worldwide Income—This is the total income or loss reported on Form 1040 before taxpayers claim the foreign-earned income and foreign housing exclusions.

It includes salaries and wages; taxable interest; dividends; taxable refunds of State and local income taxes; alimony received; business income or loss; capital gains or losses; taxable distributions from an IRA; taxable pensions and annuities; income or loss from rents, royalties, partnerships, S corporations, and estates and trusts; farm income or loss; unemployment compensation; taxable Social Security benefits, and other income or losses.

Table 1. Individual Income Tax Returns With Form 2555: Sources of Income, Deductions, Tax Items, and Foreign-Earned Income and Exclusions, by Size of Adjusted Gross Income, Tax Year 2011

[All figures are estimates based on samples—money amounts are in thousands of dollars]

Size of adjusted gross income	Total number of returns [1]	Selected income, exclusion, deduction, and credit items reported on Form 1040					
		Adjusted gross income or deficit	Worldwide income [2]	Salaries and wages		Foreign-earned income exclusion [3]	
				Number of returns	Amount	Number of returns	Amount
	(1)	(2)	(3)	(4)	(5)	(6)	(7)
All returns	**449,277**	**43,106,077**	**73,434,409**	**426,689**	**60,407,706**	**445,276**	**28,061,251**
No adjusted gross income (includes deficits)	105,777	-632,662	4,432,755	98,801	4,813,501	104,425	4,960,679
$1 under $10,000	98,095	279,925	5,564,540	92,916	5,226,686	97,718	5,178,124
$10,000 under $25,000	51,607	875,669	4,158,481	48,165	3,640,852	50,496	3,161,098
$25,000 under $50,000	50,714	1,837,429	5,539,923	48,444	4,825,124	50,519	3,514,955
$50,000 under $75,000	34,283	2,114,744	4,788,519	33,602	4,321,884	34,222	2,510,691
$75,000 under $100,000	22,551	1,944,643	3,723,551	21,599	3,266,286	22,154	1,661,268
$100,000 under $200,000	41,235	5,796,342	9,403,158	40,091	8,170,347	41,134	3,246,497
$200,000 under $500,000	29,928	9,189,865	12,218,281	28,978	10,682,610	29,658	2,487,697
$500,000 under $1,000,000	9,701	6,637,248	7,812,307	9,252	6,574,682	9,625	867,120
$1,000,000 under $1,500,000	2,494	3,012,858	3,343,277	2,220	2,503,441	2,481	220,793
$1,500,000 under $2,000,000	1,081	1,862,165	2,007,390	993	1,492,239	1,062	92,697
$2,000,000 under $5,000,000	1,359	3,980,843	4,171,922	1,210	2,723,571	1,337	119,562
$5,000,000 under $10,000,000	303	2,051,729	2,091,670	280	1,171,649	298	27,135
$10,000,000 or more	149	4,155,280	4,178,637	139	994,837	149	12,935

Size of adjusted gross income	Selected income, exclusion, deduction, and credit items reported on Form 1040—continued							
	Total adjustments		Taxable income		Foreign tax credit		Total income tax	
	Number of returns	Amount	Number of returns	Amount	Number of returns	Amount	Number of returns	Amount
	(8)	(9)	(10)	(11)	(12)	(13)	(14)	(15)
All returns	**97,612**	**688,818**	**216,961**	**36,750,497**	**107,029**	**5,737,902**	**176,124**	**5,014,836**
No adjusted gross income (includes deficits)	19,162	61,232	0	0	0	0	29	327
$1 under $10,000	15,419	39,558	1,835	1,328	401	19	1,055	115
$10,000 under $25,000	13,054	50,798	27,657	176,326	9,009	10,563	19,655	24,848
$25,000 under $50,000	14,553	77,891	45,119	798,269	15,077	50,656	32,174	118,189
$50,000 under $75,000	9,165	54,945	33,742	1,340,973	12,243	91,486	28,295	221,936
$75,000 under $100,000	6,125	39,711	22,459	1,352,591	8,948	94,611	19,492	230,387
$100,000 under $200,000	9,737	93,419	41,146	4,592,702	22,621	487,824	35,670	739,288
$200,000 under $500,000	6,537	94,180	29,917	8,112,173	24,414	1,339,910	26,158	1,101,198
$500,000 under $1,000,000	2,150	70,995	9,701	6,154,749	9,155	1,212,458	8,709	775,716
$1,000,000 under $1,500,000	735	40,802	2,494	2,826,813	2,390	549,389	2,257	374,390
$1,500,000 under $2,000,000	339	21,331	1,081	1,758,050	1,028	339,279	984	231,497
$2,000,000 under $5,000,000	457	32,416	1,359	3,764,599	1,311	716,550	1,231	487,094
$5,000,000 under $10,000,000	117	4,698	303	1,958,822	290	350,364	280	231,945
$10,000,000 or more	63	6,843	149	3,913,102	142	494,792	135	477,908

Table 1. (Continued)

Size of adjusted gross income	Selected income, exclusions, and deductions reported on Form 2555							
	Number of Forms 2555 filed by primary taxpayer	Number of Forms 2555 filed by secondary taxpayer	Total foreign-earned income		Foreign-earned income reported on Form 2555 only		Salaries and wages	
			Number of returns	Amount	Number of returns	Amount	Number of returns	Amount
	(16)	(17)	(18)	(19)	(20)	(21)	(22)	(23)
All returns	**437,127**	**51,014**	**448,728**	**54,244,646**	**346,414**	**49,176,467**	**322,841**	**37,726,589**
No adjusted gross income (includes deficits)	105,023	8,062	105,319	5,178,185	59,175	3,059,042	52,771	2,663,720
$1 under $10,000	97,482	8,269	98,144	5,413,162	66,665	3,865,008	61,719	3,514,071
$10,000 under $25,000	50,272	6,187	51,007	3,688,343	42,744	3,264,588	40,227	3,007,351
$25,000 under $50,000	47,835	7,940	50,813	4,625,324	43,136	4,206,319	40,569	3,859,526
$50,000 under $75,000	31,955	5,152	34,460	3,915,124	29,645	3,652,838	28,546	3,301,532
$75,000 under $100,000	21,240	3,097	22,386	2,907,096	20,772	2,818,341	19,706	2,550,072
$100,000 under $200,000	39,738	5,568	41,432	7,303,082	39,531	7,174,277	37,642	6,067,179
$200,000 under $500,000	28,709	4,714	30,002	9,074,786	29,686	9,037,851	28,069	6,097,203
$500,000 under $1,000,000	9,564	1,385	9,767	5,359,950	9,693	5,345,226	8,959	2,982,933
$1,000,000 under $1,500,000	2,451	315	2,506	2,004,446	2,494	1,996,993	2,148	1,063,209
$1,500,000 under $2,000,000	1,071	122	1,078	1,116,153	1,073	1,109,597	945	616,865
$2,000,000 under $5,000,000	1,339	158	1,363	2,058,124	1,353	2,053,137	1,137	1,138,957
$5,000,000 under $10,000,000	301	32	303	795,635	299	788,274	271	426,455
$10,000,000 or more	147	13	150	805,236	147	804,977	131	437,517

Size of adjusted gross income	Selected income, exclusions, and deductions reported on Form 2555—continued							
	Business or professional income (less loss)		Partnership income (less loss)		Noncash income		Allowances, reimbursements, or expenses paid by employers	
	Number of returns	Amount	Number of returns	Amount	Number of returns	Amount	Number of returns	Amount
	(24)	(25)	(26)	(27)	(28)	(29)	(30)	(31)
All returns	**28,058**	**1,979,879**	**2,621**	**1,448,735**	**13,319**	**182,889**	**45,007**	**5,226,743**
No adjusted gross income (includes deficits)	6,930	276,962	* 325	* 20,847	3,309	30,347	2,420	31,194
$1 under $10,000	6,037	214,417	* 298	* 6,576	3,245	26,672	4,698	66,456
$10,000 under $25,000	3,507	159,232	* 96	* 6,344	1,360	14,789	2,805	50,347
$25,000 under $50,000	3,494	190,696	* 51	* 3,777	1,571	21,277	3,450	89,554
$50,000 under $75,000	1,935	141,095	* 120	* 35,636	896	16,264	3,200	121,056
$75,000 under $100,000	1,403	103,398	* 41	* 3,315	387	4,737	2,043	101,878
$100,000 under $200,000	2,522	260,440	158	28,497	820	19,134	8,005	592,583
$200,000 under $500,000	1,485	309,648	490	176,359	1,144	26,526	11,452	1,735,709
$500,000 under $1,000,000	461	149,520	440	262,191	435	16,405	4,729	1,307,944
$1,000,000 under $1,500,000	120	48,476	283	232,115	86	3,908	1,138	409,469
$1,500,000 under $2,000,000	57	16,750	106	149,283	29	619	439	189,190
$2,000,000 under $5,000,000	88	71,637	170	253,529	23	697	472	306,624
$5,000,000 under $10,000,000	11	17,843	24	79,049	10	764	110	124,633
$10,000,000 or more	* 7	* 19,767	18	191,218	* 3	* 750	45	100,107

Table 1. (Continued)

Size of adjusted gross income	Selected income, exclusions, and deductions reported on Form 2555—continued									
	Less: meals and lodging excluded		Other foreign-earned income (less loss)		Foreign-earned income exclusion before deductions		Housing exclusion		Housing deduction	
	Number of returns	Amount	Number of returns	Amount	Number of returns	Amount	Number of returns	Amount	Number Of returns	Amount
	(32)	(33)	(34)	(35)	(36)	(37)	(38)	(39)	(40)	(41)
All returns	**2,576**	**31,850**	**22,351**	**2,643,482**	**447,281**	**28,344,312**	**71,599**	**1,578,263**	**5,574**	**99,010**
No adjusted gross income (includes deficits)	* 302	* 800	2,438	36,772	104,733	4,999,209	3,761	43,505	336	3,715
$1 under $10,000	822	5,347	2,433	42,163	97,969	5,234,300	5,484	66,933	332	3,594
$10,000 under $25,000	* 451	* 3,062	1,313	29,587	50,945	3,205,282	5,301	70,916	783	4,787
$25,000 under $50,000	* 317	* 3,333	1,257	44,821	50,670	3,547,245	7,920	109,649	784	8,131
$50,000 under $75,000	* 270	* 6,737	1,130	43,993	34,411	2,532,612	6,396	108,139	510	7,896
$75,000 under $100,000	* 108	* 3,745	944	58,687	22,338	1,677,456	4,555	77,930	495	5,433
$100,000 under $200,000	189	5,358	3,394	211,803	41,355	3,278,197	12,734	266,899	693	8,255
$200,000 under $500,000	95	2,943	5,461	695,348	29,793	2,511,273	15,826	446,539	637	12,392
$500,000 under $1,000,000	** 22	** 524	2,555	626,732	9,703	875,471	6,457	236,943	442	16,166

Size of adjusted gross income	Selected income, exclusions, and deductions reported on Form 2555—continued									
	Less: meals and lodging excluded		Other foreign-earned income (less loss)		Foreign-earned income exclusion before deductions		Housing exclusion		Housing deduction	
	Number of returns	Amount	Number of returns	Amount	Number of returns	Amount	Number of returns	Amount	Number Of returns	Amount
$1,000,000 under $1,500,000	0	0	677	239,816	2,496	225,201	1,563	68,825	278	13,645
$1,500,000 under $2,000,000	0	0	306	136,892	1,067	94,298	660	31,197	98	5,383
$2,000,000 under $5,000,000	0	0	329	281,694	1,353	123,116	711	39,101	152	8,051
$5,000,000 under $10,000,000	**	**	87	139,555	299	27,573	157	8,108	22	1,036
$10,000,000 or more	0	0	27	55,618	150	13,080	75	3,579	13	525

*Estimate should be used with caution because of the small number of sample returns on which it is based.

**Data combined to avoid disclosure of information for specific taxpayers. However, data are included in the appropriate totals.

[1] Includes returns with no foreign-earned income, but filed Form 2555, *Foreign Earned Income,* to claim an exclusion for a prior year or for reporting purposes.

[2] Worldwide income is total income or loss reported on Form 1040, *U.S. Individual Income Tax Return,* before the foreign-earned income and housing exclusions have been taken.

[3] Amount reported on Form 1040 is the total amount of foreign-earned income exclusion after subtracting deductions allocable to excluded income.

NOTE: Detail may not add to totals because of rounding. Data are from Forms 2555, *Foreign Earned Income,* filed by U.S. taxpayers with Form 1040, *U.S. Individual Income Tax Return.*

Source: IRS, Statistics of Income, Individual Foreign-Earned Income and Foreign Tax Credit, April 2014.

Table 2. Individual Income Tax Returns With Form 2555: Foreign-Earned Income, Exclusion Before Deductions, Housing Exclusion, and Housing Deduction, by Country or Region, Tax Year 2011
[All figures are estimates based on samples—money amounts are in thousands of dollars]

Country or region	Number of returns [1]	Total foreign-earned income	Foreign-earned income			
			Salaries and wages	Business or professional income (less loss)	Partnership income (less loss)	Noncash income
	(1)	(2)	(3)	(4)	(5)	(6)
All geographic areas	**449,277**	**54,244,646**	**37,726,589**	**1,979,879**	**1,448,735**	**182,889**
North America, total	**52,883**	**4,455,934**	**3,264,593**	**327,521**	**35,464**	**6,457**
Canada	45,949	3,841,763	2,838,767	281,626	20,783	3,180
Greenland	0	0	0	0	0	0
Mexico	6,934	614,171	425,826	45,895	* 14,681	3,277
Latin/South America, total	**14,732**	**1,757,461**	**1,070,212**	**104,699**	**132,060**	**9,188**
Argentina	986	101,199	46,560	* 5,150	* 2,888	* 2,050
Brazil	3,351	658,798	346,275	27,689	* 121,521	1,310
Chile	1,383	186,795	122,445	* 678	* 5,150	795
Colombia	1,524	169,776	123,916	* 12,467	* 1,231	* 482
Costa Rica	2,147	115,691	44,344	* 24,115	* 891	* 1,260
Panama	1,187	135,904	106,562	* 5,806	0	* 87
Peru	1,098	140,886	104,471	* 6,361	0	* 161
Venezuela	778	87,159	62,011	* 2,161	0	* 956
Other Latin and South American countries	2,280	161,252	113,629	20,272	378	2,086
Caribbean, total	**8,437**	**900,047**	**621,050**	**33,485**	*** 10,529**	**3,011**
Bermuda	1,611	375,284	281,399	* 11,871	* 1,233	* 344
Cayman Islands	1,522	112,545	59,678	* 9,273	0	* 351
Dominican Republic	678	65,941	38,884	* 4,942	* 232	* 104
Jamaica	792	54,305	29,674	* 25	* 100	* 1,039

Country or region	Number of returns [1]	Total foreign-earned income	Foreign-earned income			
			Salaries and wages	Business or professional income (less loss)	Partnership income (less loss)	Noncash income
Other Caribbean countries	3,834	291,974	211,413	* 7,375	* 8,964	* 1,171
Europe, total	**107,220**	**14,367,774**	**9,181,012**	**643,645**	**778,849**	**19,413**
Austria	1,446	135,671	81,474	* 4,792	* 672	0
Belgium	1,613	272,956	155,975	4,810	* 21,486	* 378
Czech Republic	1,318	123,737	72,741	* 7,636	* 8,893	* 1,290
Denmark	1,525	139,682	108,913	* 279	0	* 28
Finland	683	41,279	21,595	0	* 7,626	* 11
France	11,111	1,209,808	786,677	65,686	62,834	393
Germany	19,173	1,843,857	1,192,016	103,888	49,923	2,436
Greece	1,082	90,726	58,448	* 4,406	0	* 293
Hungary	428	44,915	30,566	* 3,559	* 367	* 307
Ireland	1,723	183,087	131,083	8,211	* 3,344	0
Italy	5,528	582,527	347,861	47,617	* 15,257	* 2,147
Luxembourg	521	92,352	74,249	* 341	0	0
Netherlands	3,512	533,276	317,467	7,373	* 6,065	* 636
Norway	1,336	166,735	114,207	* 957	* 1,084	* 22
Poland	756	86,888	58,047	* 3,488	* 2,377	0
Portugal	689	60,166	35,613	* 8,646	0	* 101
Russia	2,048	488,463	331,776	22,596	* 19,694	* 651
Spain	2,993	274,845	179,070	13,085	* 2,211	* 45
Sweden	1,772	161,194	115,418	* 4,164	0	* 45
Switzerland	10,548	1,832,499	1,357,515	98,325	11,514	1,933
Turkey	1,647	195,223	103,930	* 9,731	* 832	* 826
United Kingdom	31,599	5,421,593	3,279,729	185,354	563,016	5,829
Other European countries	4,170	386,296	226,641	38,705	* 1,653	* 2,044

Table 2. (Continued

Country or region	Number of returns [1]	Total foreign-earned income	Foreign-earned income			
			Salaries and wages	Business or professional income (less loss)	Partnership income (less loss)	Noncash income
	(1)	(2)	(3)	(4)	(5)	(6)
Africa, total	**14,530**	**1,588,249**	**1,058,435**	**67,476**	*** 6,641**	**4,866**
Angola	622	156,312	85,953	* 2,349	0	* 37
Egypt	1,752	238,765	172,968	* 5,778	* 2,757	* 280
Kenya	1,505	79,646	63,194	* 6,118	0	* 1,126
Morocco	491	30,419	11,535	0	0	* 7
Nigeria	1,241	234,120	120,178	* 4,592	* 1,225	* 471
South Africa	1,534	210,482	127,714	15,867	0	* 68
Other African countries	7,386	638,507	476,895	32,773	* 2,658	2,878
Asia, total	**194,703**	**24,911,137**	**17,577,987**	**607,044**	**445,465**	**114,295**
Afghanistan	22,951	2,961,433	2,652,455	104,170	0	* 2,746
China	22,328	3,267,117	2,033,969	40,468	70,395	13,441
Hong Kong	13,181	2,905,841	1,891,435	50,163	152,494	11,879
India	6,402	735,565	501,332	28,183	* 6,974	3,546
Indonesia	1,745	300,606	161,455	* 12,191	* 3,607	* 261
Iraq	14,021	1,552,010	1,350,441	22,118	0	* 416
Israel	9,872	645,902	451,668	45,656	* 9,593	* 54
Japan	23,054	2,593,308	1,570,777	44,165	90,503	6,192
Kuwait	7,481	780,878	640,581	* 13,772	* 2,547	5,273

Country or region	Number of returns [1]	Total foreign-earned income	Foreign-earned income			
			Salaries and wages	Business or professional income (less loss)	Partnership income (less loss)	Noncash income
Lebanon	2,230	147,825	114,621	* 13,727	* 145	* 1,503
Malaysia	1,405	208,115	101,042	14,581	0	* 203
Philippines	2,910	305,849	213,560	* 19,011	0	* 670
Qatar	4,205	571,297	358,203	* 8,090	* 7,896	5,503
Saudi Arabia	7,968	1,135,434	959,948	17,178	* 4,874	5,085
Singapore	7,749	1,914,293	1,235,869	17,281	23,210	11,244
South Korea	13,659	1,123,230	745,544	37,994	* 9,167	7,583
Taiwan	7,482	715,328	533,543	7,614	20,342	* 2,485
Thailand	4,205	432,292	248,496	39,300	* 1,006	2,108
United Arab Emirates	12,153	1,623,109	1,171,856	33,752	36,377	26,758
Other Asian countries	9,704	991,706	641,191	37,632	* 6,335	7,345
Oceania, total	**14,449**	**1,742,935**	**1,209,658**	**31,094**	**13,180**	**7,047**
Australia	10,353	1,443,738	974,038	27,320	13,180	4,430
New Zealand	2,563	226,704	176,561	3,744	0	* 710
Other Oceania countries	1,534	72,494	59,059	* 30	0	* 1,907
All other countries	**42,323**	**4,521,108**	**3,743,641**	**164,915**	**26,549**	**18,611**

Table 2. (Continued)

Country or region	Foreign-earned income—continued			Foreign-earned income exclusion before deductions	Housing exclusion	Housing deduction
	Allowances, reimbursements, or expenses paid by employers	Less: meals and lodging excluded	Other foreign-earned income (less loss)			
	(7)	(8)	(9)	(10)	(11)	(12)
All geographic areas	**5,226,743**	**31,850**	**2,643,482**	**28,344,312**	**1,578,263**	**99,010**
North America, total	**108,186**	*** 1,023**	**103,137**	**2,938,301**	**22,816**	**1,949**
Canada	64,665	* 1	61,210	2,580,459	14,766	1,789
Greenland	0	0	0	0	0	0
Mexico	43,521	* 1,022	41,927	357,842	8,049	* 160
Latin/South America, total	**205,444**	*** 3,760**	**89,763**	**880,165**	**31,846**	**2,577**
Argentina	20,945	0	* 3,017	56,887	2,522	0
Brazil	99,360	0	38,129	195,687	14,298	* 1,223
Chile	31,239	* 38	13,658	93,035	4,426	* 254
Colombia	11,001	0	* 10,278	105,147	3,213	0
Costa Rica	* 2,316	0	* 1,856	102,470	* 307	* 10
Panama	5,203	* 2,146	* 8,078	87,752	2,387	* 698
Peru	11,613	0	6,728	79,340	1,302	* 13
Venezuela	18,344	* 956	* 2,810	44,599	1,663	0
Other Latin and South American countries	5,424	* 620	5,207	115,247	1,729	378
Caribbean, total	**52,800**	*** 117**	**34,248**	**539,367**	**37,894**	*** 687**
Bermuda	33,290	0	21,009	138,096	28,241	* 674
Cayman Islands	* 4,447	0	* 1,965	97,601	3,143	* 1
Dominican Republic	1,676	0	* 5,391	50,393	* 390	0

Country or region	Foreign-earned income—continued			Foreign-earned income exclusion before deductions	Housing exclusion	Housing deduction
	Allowances, reimbursements, or expenses paid by employers	Less: meals and lodging excluded	Other foreign-earned income (less loss)			
Jamaica	* 278	* 12	* 509	47,887	* 26	0
Other Caribbean countries	13,110	* 105	* 5,374	205,394	6,093	* 13
Europe, total	**1,496,297**	*** 2,226**	**871,562**	**6,668,589**	**447,264**	**35,879**
Austria	10,352	0	* 921	97,363	2,523	* 116
Belgium	49,828	* 30	30,713	124,682	13,001	* 252
Czech Republic	17,057	0	10,299	70,147	1,423	* 222
Denmark	* 2,042	0	* 3,537	106,224	883	* 10
Finland	* 2,251	0	* 2,164	26,439	* 227	* 68
France	114,962	* 4	44,191	623,621	53,453	4,229
Germany	121,908	0	77,510	1,101,969	50,701	5,704
Greece	* 1,788	0	* 238	64,613	1,445	0
Hungary	* 5,819	0	* 1,832	21,621	* 878	0
Ireland	8,953	0	12,904	98,620	3,581	* 214
Italy	69,033	0	37,296	319,520	16,636	1,067
Luxembourg	* 1,352	0	11,944	42,776	2,842	* 251
Netherlands	111,856	0	36,350	257,283	18,194	* 20
Norway	14,061	0	5,283	99,775	2,680	* 24
Poland	8,102	0	7,109	38,627	2,358	* 13
Portugal	0	* 57	* 8,072	48,627	* 398	* 37
Russia	56,737	0	37,190	137,514	29,876	2,613
Spain	14,171	0	17,752	153,266	10,228	* 39
Sweden	8,052	0	* 1,769	115,135	2,354	0
Switzerland	161,170	* 647	115,226	834,680	69,010	3,245
Turkey	36,158	0	11,677	102,168	3,912	* 162
United Kingdom	649,332	* 21	388,128	1,944,761	153,213	17,090
Other European countries	31,314	* 1,467	9,453	239,158	7,451	* 503

Table 2. (Continued)

Country or region	Foreign-earned income—continued			Foreign-earned income exclusion before deductions	Housing exclusion	Housing deduction
	Allowances, reimbursements, or expenses paid by employers	Less: meals and lodging excluded	Other foreign-earned income (less loss)			
	(7)	(8)	(9)	(10)	(11)	(12)
Africa, total	**259,439**	*** 1,346**	**81,886**	**839,441**	**33,650**	**2,341**
Angola	59,755	0	7,871	48,570	9,341	0
Egypt	35,634	* 93	* 11,312	114,203	3,701	* 617
Kenya	* 2,679	* 1,101	* 2,010	57,790	1,749	* 14
Morocco	* 1,412	0	* 956	24,287	* 248	0
Nigeria	79,667	0	7,229	89,842	2,319	* 13
South Africa	32,868	0	25,799	96,921	4,167	* 18
Other African countries	47,423	* 152	26,710	407,829	12,127	* 1,679
Asia, total	**2,797,480**	**20,044**	**1,330,596**	**12,730,672**	**923,406**	**47,189**
Afghanistan	6,819	* 2,917	* 2,334	1,749,519	3,220	* 254
China	629,455	4,055	276,667	1,444,917	137,003	5,610
Hong Kong	408,145	* 532	261,570	975,487	232,093	11,677
India	89,008	* 717	57,469	388,602	13,790	183
Indonesia	91,112	0	16,202	113,944	7,425	0
Iraq	* 9,718	0	* 180	1,029,197	2,757	* 150
Israel	9,161	0	8,631	488,073	2,515	* 146
Japan	307,977	* 564	255,376	1,246,605	141,647	13,963
Kuwait	23,208	* 1,218	* 4,836	575,054	17,014	* 557
Lebanon	* 8,709	0	* 1,215	124,862	* 984	* 16

Country or region	Foreign-earned income—continued			Foreign-earned income exclusion before deductions	Housing exclusion	Housing deduction
	Allowances, reimbursements, or expenses paid by employers	Less: meals and lodging excluded	Other foreign-earned income (less loss)			
Malaysia	75,213	0	12,262	79,825	7,712	* 14
Philippines	35,759	0	17,150	168,519	6,966	* 269
Qatar	113,208	* 1,843	14,951	322,587	22,200	* 801
Saudi Arabia	62,534	* 258	12,027	598,546	9,095	980
Singapore	381,621	* 104	213,001	634,166	153,308	3,123
South Korea	121,134	* 3,345	45,789	656,363	33,895	1,764
Taiwan	35,004	0	22,351	417,302	10,750	* 390
Thailand	90,096	0	13,500	227,775	11,908	483
United Arab Emirates	158,196	* 3,471	56,662	905,731	89,278	5,738
Other Asian countries	141,404	* 1,020	38,422	583,597	19,847	1,070
Oceania, total	**219,851**	*** 2,481**	**79,470**	**954,874**	**34,444**	**556**
Australia	218,237	* 404	78,759	707,197	32,469	441
New Zealand	* 454	0	* 712	181,218	1,970	* 107
Other Oceania countries	1,161	* 2,076	0	66,458	* 5	* 8
All other countries	**87,246**	**852**	**52,819**	**2,792,904**	**46,944**	**7,833**

* Estimate should be used with caution because of the small number of sample returns on which it is based.

[1] Includes returns with no foreign-earned income, but filed Form 2555 to claim an exclusion for a prior year or for reporting purposes.

NOTE: Detail may not add to totals because of rounding. Data are from Forms 2555, *Foreign Earned Income,* filed by U.S. taxpayers with Form 1040, *U.S. Individual Income Tax Return.*

Source: IRS, Statistics of Income, Individual Foreign-Earned Income and Foreign Tax Credit, April 2014.

Table 3. Individual Income Tax Returns With a Foreign Tax Credit or a Form 1116: Sources of Income, Deductions and Tax Items, and Foreign Income, Taxes, and Credit, by Size of Adjusted Gross Income, Tax Year 2011

[All figures are estimates based on samples--money amounts are in thousands of dollars]

Size of adjusted gross income	Number of returns [1]	Selected income, exclusion, deduction, and credit items reported on Form 1040						
		Adjusted gross income or deficit	Worldwide income [2]		Salaries and wages		Foreign-earned income exclusion [3]	
			Number of returns	Amount	Number of returns	Amount	Number of returns	Amount
	(1)	(2)	(3)	(4)	(5)	(6)	(7)	(8)
All returns	**8,065,020**	**1,758,261,571**	**8,065,016**	**1,803,299,777**	**5,394,247**	**862,273,355**	**141,438**	**10,991,801**
No adjusted gross income (includes deficits)	181,378	-60,718,996	181,374	-59,858,704	54,458	3,619,008	7,787	404,596
$1 under $10,000	291,945	1,382,352	291,945	2,301,536	122,358	1,354,476	13,100	779,502
$10,000 under $25,000	563,705	10,061,586	563,705	11,380,781	238,928	4,394,808	14,197	938,365
$25,000 under $50,000	1,028,019	38,927,994	1,028,019	41,567,598	544,622	17,490,731	18,874	1,484,168
$50,000 under $75,000	1,145,759	71,648,271	1,145,759	74,222,561	684,444	33,125,727	13,695	1,091,036
$75,000 under $100,000	1,055,408	92,250,401	1,055,408	94,862,653	700,750	47,075,864	9,972	817,752
$100,000 under $200,000	2,055,774	289,593,370	2,055,774	297,534,589	1,573,974	172,228,122	24,183	2,021,271
$200,000 under $500,000	1,214,954	365,217,580	1,214,954	376,305,084	1,034,808	232,438,972	25,251	2,159,301
$500,000 under $1,000,000	321,338	219,839,034	321,338	225,902,650	271,347	123,848,691	9,220	836,086
$1,000,000 under $1,500,000	87,211	105,953,545	87,211	108,274,916	71,500	50,396,960	2,398	214,462
$1,500,000 under $2,000,000	37,555	64,543,219	37,555	65,712,771	30,415	27,972,649	1,025	90,000
$2,000,000 under $5,000,000	57,238	171,756,306	57,238	174,189,936	46,438	65,571,696	1,303	116,171
$5,000,000 under $10,000,000	15,045	102,789,079	15,045	103,789,194	12,399	34,010,736	288	26,338
$10,000,000 or more	9,690	285,017,830	9,690	287,114,212	7,807	48,744,916	146	12,754

Size of adjusted gross income	Selected income, exclusion, deduction, and credit items reported on Form 1040—Continued							
	Foreign housing deduction		Taxable income		Foreign tax credit		Total income tax	
	Number of returns	Amount	Number of returns	Amount	Number of returns	Amount	Number of returns	Amount
	(9)	(10)	(11)	(12)	(13)	(14)	(15)	(16)
All returns	**2,778**	**67,229**	**7,471,819**	**1,452,572,118**	**6,904,438**	**16,451,088**	**7,047,214**	**340,706,955**
No adjusted gross income (includes deficits)	**36	**139	0	0	* 59	* 7	897	56,853
$1 under $10,000	**	**	105,290	224,216	64,717	2,927	72,033	28,794
$10,000 under $25,000	* 218	* 619	420,018	2,935,828	347,554	31,528	312,293	204,262
$25,000 under $50,000	184	1,063	982,277	20,543,889	879,375	162,771	840,132	1,921,264
$50,000 under $75,000	281	3,191	1,132,487	46,415,606	1,051,447	245,067	1,067,412	5,688,386
$75,000 under $100,000	196	2,702	1,049,172	64,557,185	988,734	272,407	1,019,099	8,645,520
$100,000 under $200,000	367	5,339	2,045,226	216,579,546	1,933,133	1,204,407	2,007,569	36,563,085
$200,000 under $500,000	524	10,198	1,211,203	292,758,715	1,142,539	3,071,156	1,203,511	71,138,045
$500,000 under $1,000,000	419	15,571	320,064	184,213,064	302,252	2,542,393	318,884	51,789,893
$1,000,000 under $1,500,000	267	13,410	86,911	90,260,042	81,708	1,331,248	86,595	25,609,516
$1,500,000 under $2,000,000	98	5,383	37,434	55,135,930	35,636	835,052	37,289	15,748,151
$2,000,000 under $5,000,000	152	8,051	57,077	147,721,726	53,958	2,087,824	56,881	41,848,159
$5,000,000 under $10,000,000	22	1,036	15,003	88,734,914	14,187	1,177,830	14,976	24,309,171
$10,000,000 or more	13	525	9,657	242,491,457	9,139	3,486,470	9,644	57,155,855

Table 3. (Continued)

Size of adjusted gross income	Returns with a Form 1116							
	Foreign income, taxes and credit reported on Form 1116							
	Foreign-source gross income		Foreign-source deductions and losses		Foreign-source taxable income before adjustments [4]		Foreign taxes paid or accrued on: Total	
	Number of returns	Amount	Number of returns	Amount	Number of returns	Amount	Number of returns	Amount
	(17)	(18)	(19)	(20)	(21)	(22)	(23)	(24)
All returns	**3,575,251**	**169,982,715**	**3,443,372**	**70,628,235**	**3,583,324**	**99,354,480**	**3,366,547**	**22,039,411**
No adjusted gross income (includes deficits)	138,644	7,034,246	133,929	6,225,658	141,067	808,588	130,051	242,676
$1 under $10,000	207,402	514,699	203,137	364,303	208,065	150,396	190,117	96,264
$10,000 under $25,000	279,331	1,902,940	271,769	1,146,176	280,256	756,764	261,797	212,027
$25,000 under $50,000	404,393	3,017,088	393,306	706,324	406,168	2,310,764	377,909	448,600
$50,000 under $75,000	421,035	3,050,756	406,310	583,037	421,441	2,467,719	391,814	515,090
$75,000 under $100,000	365,695	3,130,087	349,557	561,357	366,023	2,568,730	344,774	449,483
$100,000 under $200,000	775,745	10,848,511	738,108	1,593,917	776,291	9,254,594	728,925	2,004,294
$200,000 under $500,000	616,633	21,818,891	590,575	4,371,238	617,383	17,447,653	584,811	4,278,987
$500,000 under $1,000,000	206,798	17,350,289	200,855	5,096,068	206,806	12,254,221	200,076	3,290,831
$1,000,000 under $1,500,000	63,309	9,360,918	61,626	2,880,718	63,449	6,480,200	61,610	1,724,656
$1,500,000 under $2,000,000	28,459	6,928,603	27,827	2,846,243	28,483	4,082,360	27,890	1,013,409
$2,000,000 under $5,000,000	46,036	18,631,956	44,982	7,406,767	46,099	11,225,189	45,271	2,515,536
$5,000,000 under $10,000,000	12,931	13,035,646	12,682	6,065,264	12,949	6,970,382	12,734	1,360,852
$10,000,000 or more	8,839	53,358,084	8,710	30,781,164	8,845	22,576,920	8,767	3,886,706

Size of adjusted gross income	Returns with a Form 1116—continued							
	Foreign income, taxes and credit reported on Form 1116—continued							
	Foreign taxes paid or accrued on:—continued							
	Dividends		Rents and royalties		Interest		Other income	
	Number of returns	Amount	Number of returns	Amount	Number of returns	Amount	Number of returns	Amount
	(25)	(26)	(27)	(28)	(29)	(30)	(31)	(32)
All returns	**2,878,341**	**2,223,581**	**25,151**	**166,865**	**80,196**	**240,054**	**721,330**	**19,408,912**
No adjusted gross income (includes deficits)	115,145	55,866	460	3,953	1,677	1,087	21,892	181,770
$1 under $10,000	166,460	10,775	* 741	* 3,169	1,419	390	27,418	81,931
$10,000 under $25,000	219,645	26,088	* 1,270	* 1,645	5,274	4,778	46,767	179,515
$25,000 under $50,000	312,918	48,558	2,207	2,246	8,434	12,017	78,525	385,779
$50,000 under $75,000	338,491	69,272	2,689	6,948	6,081	3,523	67,983	435,348
$75,000 under $100,000	304,962	79,322	1,468	1,880	7,498	5,407	55,079	362,875
$100,000 under $200,000	620,080	301,316	4,976	16,993	15,965	16,179	144,082	1,669,805
$200,000 under $500,000	500,500	353,950	7,010	40,704	21,493	20,501	142,020	3,863,832
$500,000 under $1,000,000	169,293	243,900	2,354	24,967	6,484	29,879	64,587	2,992,085
$1,000,000 under $1,500,000	52,063	137,267	692	8,370	1,970	6,121	24,720	1,572,898
$1,500,000 under $2,000,000	23,381	90,812	289	4,287	1,104	3,468	12,492	914,842
$2,000,000 under $5,000,000	38,114	220,540	691	17,113	1,879	20,500	22,608	2,257,382
$5,000,000 under $10,000,000	10,459	144,240	167	17,761	519	7,487	7,252	1,191,366
$10,000,000 or more	6,832	441,676	139	16,829	401	108,718	5,904	3,319,483

Table 3. (Continued)

Size of adjusted gross income	Returns with a Form 1116—continued									
	Foreign income, taxes and credit reported on Form 1116—continued									
	Foreign taxes available for credit		Foreign tax carryover		Reduction in foreign taxes		Gross foreign tax credit		Foreign tax credit after adjustments [5]	
	Number of returns	Amount	Number of returns	Amount	Number of returns	Amount	Number of returns	Amount	Number of returns	Amount
	(33)	(34)	(35)	(36)	(37)	(38)	(39)	(40)	(41)	(42)
All returns	**3,746,457**	**33,821,904**	**1,577,864**	**13,735,047**	**88,754**	**1,974,191**	**2,758,322**	**16,180,506**	**2,761,046**	**16,164,689**
No adjusted gross income (includes deficits)	175,523	1,215,057	127,615	995,258	3,342	24,215	* 44	* 6	* 44	* 6
$1 under $10,000	241,495	163,718	156,195	122,015	5,202	58,198	26,496	1,551	26,496	1,551
$10,000 under $25,000	316,983	530,508	196,122	400,698	5,710	82,217	114,620	24,040	114,620	23,947
$25,000 under $50,000	428,115	730,058	236,681	434,110	8,841	153,541	301,932	138,276	301,921	137,671
$50,000 under $75,000	437,232	779,499	185,809	408,228	7,736	143,857	362,683	211,889	363,680	211,424
$75,000 under $100,000	376,538	676,279	135,282	334,931	5,903	109,238	329,410	234,987	330,381	234,087
$100,000 under $200,000	786,179	2,916,247	264,151	1,306,386	16,456	391,294	705,138	1,119,482	705,239	1,117,927
$200,000 under $500,000	616,978	6,692,379	175,258	2,930,243	21,047	529,116	572,746	3,022,388	572,898	3,016,545
$500,000 under $1,000,000	207,398	4,717,409	57,812	1,691,005	8,656	264,749	194,201	2,528,818	194,622	2,526,746
$1,000,000 under $1,500,000	63,337	2,474,729	17,712	823,355	2,387	75,480	59,497	1,324,762	59,513	1,326,892
$1,500,000 under $2,000,000	28,524	1,544,885	7,292	564,155	1,061	33,159	27,132	833,437	27,156	832,607
$2,000,000 under $5,000,000	46,272	3,872,573	12,130	1,401,277	1,567	45,087	43,705	2,083,088	43,742	2,082,823
$5,000,000 under $10,000,000	12,988	2,029,181	3,314	682,510	460	14,949	12,309	1,172,153	12,320	1,171,342
$10,000,000 or more	8,895	5,479,381	2,492	1,640,875	387	49,091	8,411	3,485,628	8,416	3,481,123

* Estimate should be used with caution because of the small number of sample returns on which it is based.

** Data combined to prevent disclosure of taxpayer information.

[1] Not all taxpayers with a foreign tax credit file the Form 1116, *Foreign Tax Credit.* Taxpayers with $300 ($600 if married filing a joint return) or less in creditable foreign taxes who also meet certain other conditions are not required to file Form 1116 to claim the foreign tax credit.

[2] Worldwide income is total income or loss reported on Form 1040, *U.S. Individual Income Tax Return,* before the foreign-earned income and housing exclusions have been taken.

[3] Amount reported on Form 1040 is the total amount of foreign-earned income exclusion after subtracting deductions allocable to excluded income.

[4] Adjustments include allocation of foreign and U.S. losses, recapture of prior-year foreign losses, and recharacterization of income.

[5] Adjustments include reductions for participation in unsanctioned international boycotts and increases permitted by tax treaties between the United States and certain foreign countries.

NOTES: Detail may not add to totals because of rounding. Data are from Forms 1116, *Foreign Tax Credit,* which U.S. taxpayers file with Form 1040, *U.S. Individual Income Tax Return.*

Source: IRS, Statistics of Income, Individual Foreign-Earned Income and Foreign Tax Credit, April 2014.

Table 4. Individual Income Tax Returns With Form 1116: Foreign-Source Income, Deductions, and Taxes, by Country or Region, Tax Year 2011

[All figures are estimates based on samples—money amounts are in thousands of dollars]

Country or region	Number of returns	Foreign-source gross income	Foreign-taxable source deductions and losses	Foreign-source income before adjustments [1]	Foreign taxes paid or accrued on:				
					Total	Dividends	Rents and royalties	Interest	Other income
	(1)	(2)	(3)	(4)	(5)	(6)	(7)	(8)	(9)
All geographic areas	**3,921,628**	**169,982,715**	**70,628,235**	**99,354,480**	**22,039,411**	**2,223,581**	**166,865**	**240,054**	**19,408,912**
North America, total	**442,718**	**16,652,533**	**6,293,190**	**10,359,344**	**2,778,640**	**182,469**	**39,471**	**20,417**	**2,536,283**
Canada	405,886	12,934,181	4,232,307	8,701,874	2,414,016	153,629	24,957	19,497	2,215,932
Mexico	36,827	3,718,006	2,060,862	1,657,144	364,501	28,839	14,514	920	320,228
Other North American countries	* 5	* 347	* 21	* 326	* 123	0	0	0	* 123
Latin/South America, total	**31,961**	**7,202,573**	**4,931,331**	**2,271,242**	**651,001**	**40,016**	**3,538**	**4,613**	**602,834**
Argentina	3,128	197,403	53,656	143,747	34,034	381	* 198	0	33,456
Brazil	18,052	1,421,725	330,261	1,091,465	279,093	8,162	3,116	4,036	263,779
Chile	2,058	493,583	376,094	117,489	61,691	774	0	* 15	60,902
Colombia	3,821	4,316,293	4,014,744	301,549	135,133	633	* 67	336	134,097
Costa Rica	341	25,974	17,113	8,861	2,509	* 3	* 3	* 13	2,490
Panama	432	114,679	25,463	89,216	12,764	* 66	* 52	* 1	12,645
Peru	2,025	241,355	31,406	209,950	31,656	672	* 23	* 130	30,832
Venezuela	962	203,105	29,270	173,835	56,439	* 29,036	0	0	27,404
Other Latin/South American countries	1,145	188,456	53,324	135,132	37,683	289	* 81	* 82	37,231
Caribbean, total	**9,197**	**1,023,967**	**170,672**	**853,295**	**73,322**	**14,632**	*** 111**	*** 64**	**58,516**
Bermuda	1,540	193,198	27,184	166,014	4,516	168	* [2]	0	4,348
Cayman Islands	1,607	277,009	19,035	257,974	1,952	* [2]	* 2	0	1,950
Dominican Republic	196	35,453	3,945	31,508	6,146	* 49	* 55	0	6,042

Country or region	Number of returns	Foreign-source gross income	Foreign-taxable source deductions and losses	Foreign-source income before adjustments [1]	Foreign taxes paid or accrued on:				
					Total	Dividends	Rents and royalties	Interest	Other income
Jamaica	735	104,481	49,376	55,105	16,696	* 8,309	0	* 58	8,328
Other Caribbean countries	5,118	413,826	71,134	342,694	44,014	6,105	* 53	* 6	37,847
Europe, total	**393,233**	**32,365,839**	**8,489,532**	**23,876,307**	**8,305,468**	**393,232**	**54,548**	**142,029**	**7,715,659**
Austria	2,412	195,493	90,735	104,758	35,335	1,546	* 115	201	33,473
Belgium	5,553	437,335	127,751	309,584	133,914	11,240	* 3	58	122,613
Czech Republic	475	91,820	16,904	74,916	13,889	* 1,799	* 2	55	12,033
Denmark	5,527	368,399	156,804	211,595	72,774	4,647	* 1	* 236	67,889
Finland	10,768	66,137	6,565	59,572	15,042	2,298	* 2	19	12,724
France	53,858	1,894,704	615,101	1,279,603	311,276	12,563	6,515	586	291,611
Germany	55,654	5,557,019	2,812,842	2,744,178	1,058,811	83,931	3,784	9,309	961,787
Greece	2,813	259,270	52,971	206,299	48,202	* 245	2,721	296	44,939
Hungary	316	223,607	138,251	85,356	19,134	* 2,879	* 39	* 12	16,204
Ireland	5,508	411,330	65,547	345,783	133,983	894	* 760	121	132,207
Italy	7,881	652,651	150,262	502,389	200,262	12,862	15,605	331	171,464
Luxembourg	7,459	670,717	30,299	640,418	110,969	68,005	* 120	* 29	42,814
Netherlands	19,467	987,306	254,802	732,505	218,123	16,434	* 586	249	200,854
Norway	6,509	353,402	51,836	301,566	85,149	1,950	* 4,371	784	78,043
Poland	1,170	198,068	82,050	116,019	34,708	1,326	* 30	131	33,220
Portugal	779	37,396	4,631	32,765	8,205	27	* 35	* 125	8,017
Russia	2,577	1,216,501	330,355	886,146	173,232	21,314	* 914	377	150,628
Spain	16,094	418,019	49,790	368,229	100,301	12,985	104	708	86,504
Sweden	12,692	472,749	89,533	383,216	105,396	20,852	* 110	175	84,258
Switzerland	24,127	3,299,242	316,677	2,982,565	880,575	46,466	7,834	112,673	713,602
Turkey	613	199,262	16,065	183,197	52,128	1,590	429	472	49,638
United Kingdom	135,324	13,887,534	2,916,872	10,970,662	4,440,803	59,563	9,635	15,042	4,356,562
Other European countries	15,656	467,875	112,890	354,989	53,258	7,816	* 833	36	44,574

Footnotes at end of table.

Table 4. (Continued)

Country or region	Number of returns	Foreign-source gross income	Foreign-source deductions and losses	Foreign- source taxable income before adjustments [1]	Foreign taxes paid or accrued on:				
					Total	Dividends	Rents and royalties	Interest	Other income
	(1)	(2)	(3)	(4)	(5)	(6)	(7)	(8)	(9)
Africa, total	**10,535**	**1,940,849**	**237,593**	**1,703,257**	**439,534**	**1,495**	*** 1,647**	**1,568**	**434,824**
Angola	1,365	391,589	23,340	368,249	60,809	* 47	0	0	60,763
Egypt	672	183,397	8,212	175,185	46,450	68	0	0	46,382
Kenya	93	13,146	6,002	7,144	2,114	* [2]	* 15	* 21	2,079
Morocco	59	8,682	2,124	6,558	2,843	0	0	0	2,843
Nigeria	1,780	506,833	43,094	463,738	69,992	* 8	0	0	69,985
South Africa	2,165	382,845	84,840	298,005	160,015	744	* 541	* 120	158,609
Other African countries	4,402	454,357	69,983	384,377	97,310	628	* 1,091	* 1,428	94,162
Asia, total	**182,776**	**19,093,930**	**2,964,048**	**16,129,883**	**4,177,757**	**147,418**	**30,055**	**32,767**	**3,967,518**
Afghanistan	2,403	104,892	28,005	76,886	13,740	89	0	* 131	13,520
China	27,027	3,935,103	818,828	3,116,275	981,874	14,734	1,416	1,404	964,321
Hong Kong	10,457	2,660,033	397,229	2,262,804	395,809	3,807	790	* 206	391,007
India	28,657	1,841,732	274,453	1,567,279	462,874	10,030	14,089	19,427	419,328
Indonesia	1,929	393,580	22,515	371,065	104,507	497	* 12	129	* 103,869
Iraq	484	81,650	33,425	48,225	* 584	0	0	0	* 584
Israel	21,331	841,584	108,313	733,271	257,029	37,478	547	3,025	215,979
Japan	48,202	3,115,052	503,691	2,611,361	861,206	9,213	1,748	1,240	849,005
Kuwait	191	26,594	2,398	24,196	* 1	* 1	0	0	0
Lebanon	1,138	53,952	14,559	39,393	3,324	* 77	0	* 2,045	1,202
Malaysia	1,412	260,747	38,597	222,150	57,012	220	* 172	0	56,620
Philippines	3,373	223,548	19,426	204,122	54,291	5,995	* 2,097	27	46,172

Country or region	Number of returns	Foreign-source gross income	Foreign-source deductions and losses	Foreign- source taxable income before adjustments [1]	Foreign taxes paid or accrued on:				
					Total	Dividends	Rents and royalties	Interest	Other income
Qatar	732	187,843	40,366	147,477	9,187	* 17	0	0	9,170
Saudi Arabia	961	244,967	31,611	213,356	12,685	* 79	0	* [2]	12,607
Singapore	9,168	2,017,640	226,653	1,790,987	349,718	13,085	690	* 46	335,897
South Korea	8,811	898,763	125,434	773,329	160,839	10,854	6,715	4,720	138,550
Taiwan	6,401	708,351	81,555	626,796	191,255	39,503	1,132	238	150,382
Thailand	1,980	355,725	36,949	318,777	110,180	717	* 24	28	109,410
United Arab Emirates	2,394	353,006	49,557	303,450	4,390	102	0	0	4,288
Other Asian countries	5,725	789,170	110,481	678,685	147,250	920	621	100	145,607
Oceania, total	**30,662**	**2,682,217**	**604,963**	**2,077,255**	**645,055**	**12,055**	**4,337**	**13,153**	**615,510**
Australia	22,391	2,398,005	516,561	1,881,444	598,001	10,418	3,938	9,112	574,532
New Zealand	6,901	241,949	71,468	170,481	44,029	1,615	* 399	4,034	37,982
Other Oceania countries	1,369	42,264	16,934	25,331	3,025	* 22	0	* 7	2,996
U.S. Possessions, total	**31,285**	**1,430,502**	**348,711**	**1,081,791**	**165,772**	**2,989**	*** 78**	*** 438**	**162,267**
Puerto Rico	29,700	1,309,533	269,338	1,040,196	156,105	1,116	* 78	0	154,910
Other U.S. Possessions	1,585	120,969	79,373	41,594	9,667	* 1,872	0	* 438	7,357
Country not stated	**3,503,482**	**87,494,522**	**46,560,248**	**40,934,274**	**4,798,598**	**1,427,472**	**33,072**	**24,557**	**3,313,497**
High taxed [3]	**106,047**	**95,783**	**27,949**	**67,834**	**4,261**	**1,803**	*** 8**	**448**	**2,003**

* Estimate should be used with caution because of the small number of sample returns on which it is based.

[1] Adjustments include allocation of foreign and U.S. losses, recapture of prior-year foreign losses, and recharacterization of income.

[2] Less than $500.

[3] High taxed is passive category income and taxes treated as general category income and taxes because the foreign taxes paid on the income (after expenses) exceeds the highest U.S. tax that can be imposed on the income.

NOTES: Detail may not add to totals because of rounding. Data are from Forms 1116, *Foreign Tax Credit,* which U.S. taxpayers file with Form 1040, *U.S. Individual Income Tax Return.*

Source: IRS, Statistics of Income, Individual Foreign-Earned Income and Foreign Tax Credit, April 2014.

Table 5. Individual Income Tax Returns With Form 1116: Foreign-Source Income, Deductions, and Taxes, by Type of Income, Tax Year 2011

[All figures are estimates based on samples--money amounts are in thousands of dollars]

Type of income	Number of returns [1]	Foreign-source gross income		Foreign-source deductions and losses	
		Number of returns	Amount	Number of returns	Amount
	(1)	(2)	(3)	(4)	(5)
All returns	**3,921,628**	**3,576,909**	**169,982,715**	**3,444,866**	**70,628,235**
Passive income [4]	2,983,396	2,722,673	47,923,175	2,615,314	13,762,424
General limitation income [5]	1,213,622	1,065,050	121,378,748	1,035,268	56,666,713
Section 901(j) income [6]	243	191	63,966	51	93,933
Certain income re-sourced by treaty [7]	10,059	9,726	593,721	9,371	103,586
Lump-sum distributions [8]	3,689	1,075	23,105	1,072	1,580

Type of income	Foreign-source taxable income before adjustments [2]		Foreign taxes paid or accrued on:					
			Total		Dividends		Rents and royalties	
	Number of returns	Amount	Number of returns	Amount	Number of returns	Amount	Number of returns	Amount
	(6)	(7)	(8)	(9)	(10)	(11)	(12)	(13)
All returns	**3,584,450**	**99,354,480**	**3,366,548**	**22,039,411**	**2,878,342**	**2,223,581**	**25,151**	**166,865**
Passive income [4]	2,724,505	34,160,751	2,545,713	3,831,812	2,329,866	1,745,594	16,153	82,823
General limitation income [5]	1,075,038	64,712,035	957,534	18,079,872	561,944	474,719	9,010	83,569
Section 901(j) income [6]	192	-29,967	60	1,421	* 43	* 1	0	0
Certain income re-sourced by treaty [7]	9,729	490,135	9,521	120,240	** 2,482	** 3,267	** 61	** 473
Lump-sum distributions [8]	1,075	21,525	1,290	6,065	**	**	**	**
Type of income	Foreign taxes paid or accrued on:				Foreign taxes available		Gross foreign tax credit [3]	

	Interest		Other income		for credit			
	Number of returns	Amount	Number of returns	Amount	Number of returns	Amount	Number of returns	Amount
	(14)	(15)	(16)	(17)	(18)	(19)	(20)	(21)
All returns	**80,196**	**240,054**	**721,330**	**19,408,912**	**3,746,457**	**33,821,904**	**2,758,322**	**16,180,506**
Passive income [4]	72,043	210,837	333,636	1,792,558	2,803,084	6,659,664	2,049,520	2,787,237
General limitation income [5]	7,236	27,358	425,592	17,494,226	1,129,560	26,969,980	822,593	13,298,489
Section 901(j) income [6]	**	**	**	**	64	4,164	0	0
Certain income re-sourced by treaty [7]	** 1,805	** 1,856	** 7,644	** 116,092	9,813	180,635	8,939	91,312
Lump-sum distributions [8]	0	0	1,239	6,036	3,688	7,461	1,082	3,467

* Estimate should be used with caution because of the small number of sample returns on which it is based.

** Data combined to prevent disclosure of taxpayer information.

[1] Taxpayers may report more than one type of foreign-source income on a return. Consequently, the number of returns by type of income do not add to total.

[2] Adjustments include allocation of foreign and U.S. losses, recapture of prior-year foreign losses, and recharacterization of income.

[3] This is before adjustments. Adjustments include reductions for participation in unsanctioned international boycotts and increases permitted by tax treaties between the United States and certain foreign countries.

[4] Passive income generally includes dividends, interest, rents, royalties, and annuities.

[5] General limitation income is foreign income from sources outside the United States that do not fall into one of the other four categories; it includes high-taxed income that would otherwise be passive income.

[6] Section 901(j) income is income earned from activities conducted in a sanctioned country. No credit is allowed for taxes paid or accrued to sanctioned countries, which for 2011 were Cuba, Iran, North Korea, Sudan, and Syria.

[7] Certain income re-sourced by treaty allows specific types of income to be treated as foreign-source income, if there is a tax treaty that treats it as such, and the treaty is applied.

[8] Lump-sum distributions are distributions from a retirement plan that are subject to U.S. tax using income averaging.

NOTES: Detail may not add to totals because of rounding. Data are from Forms 1116, *Foreign Tax Credit,* which U.S. taxpayers file with Form 1040, *U.S. Individual Income Tax Return.*

Source: IRS, Statistics of Income, Individual Foreign-Earned Income and Foreign Tax Credit, April 2014.

End Notes

[1] Data for all taxpayers who filed a Form 1040 for 2011 cited in this article are from *Statistics of Income, Individual Income Tax Returns 2011*, Publication 1304.

[2] Data in this article are compared to 2006 and 2001 data because these are the last years for which comparable statistics are available.

[3] For comparability, 2006 amounts presented in this article were adjusted for U.S. inflation to 2011 constant dollars. However, these adjustments do not necessarily adjust for country-specific inflation in countries for which income was reported. The inflation-adjusted constant-dollar amounts are based on the Consumer Price Index (CPI-U) computed and reported by the U.S. Department of Labor, Bureau of Labor Statistics, *Monthly Labor Review*. The consumer price index represents annual averages of monthly indices and approximates buying patterns of typical urban consumers.

Year	CPI-U
2011	224.939
2006	201.6

[4] See Hollenbeck, Scott, and Maureen Keenan Kahr. "Individual Foreign-Earned Income and Foreign Tax Credit, 2006," *Statistics of Income Bulletin,* Spring 2009, Volume 28, Number 4.

[5] A foreign tax credit is not allowed for foreign taxes paid or accrued to countries sanctioned by the U.S. Government. Nevertheless, a foreign tax credit limitation is computed for each sanctioned country. For 2011, the countries were Cuba, Iran, North Korea, Sudan, and Syria.

[6] For income from the certain income re-sourced by treaty category, a separate foreign tax credit limitation has to be computed for each amount re-sourced from a treaty country.

[7] Taxpayers with $300 ($600 if married filing a joint return) or less in creditable foreign taxes, who met certain other conditions, mainly that the foreign-source gross income was from the passive income category, and all of the income and any foreign taxes paid on it were reported on a qualified payee statement, did not have to file Form 1116 to claim the foreign tax credit on Form 1040. Also, some taxpayers deduct their foreign taxes on Schedule A rather than taking a credit by filing Form 1116. Therefore, foreign-source income for these taxpayers would not be reported.

[8] The $87.6 billion of total foreign-source gross income reported without a stated country includes $0.1 billion for high-taxed income.

[9] The $4.8 billion of total foreign taxes paid or accrued without a stated country includes $4.3 million in taxes paid or accrued on high-taxed income.

[10] As stipulated on Form 1116, *Foreign Tax Credit*, Part III Figuring the Credit.

INDEX

D

E

J

K

L

M

N

O

P

Q

R

S

T

U

V

W